THE JOYCE WE KNEW

The Joyce we Knew

Edited by
ULICK O'CONNOR

Memoirs by
EUGENE SHEEHY

WILLIAM G. FALLON

PÁDRAIC COLUM

ARTHUR POWER

THE MERCIER PRESS
4 BRIDGE STREET, CORK

CONTENTS

INTRODUCTION

James Joyce was born in 1882. The four contributors to this book were born within a year or two of this date. Eugene Sheehy and William Fallon knew James Joyce as a schoolboy in Belvedere. Padraic Colum knew him in his student years, and Arthur Power first met Joyce when he had become a famous writer in Paris in the twenties.

The first surprise is to find out how much of an extrovert Joyce was. He is the practical joker in the school drama society and in the gymnasium. He is the star when they play charades at genteel Dublin musical evenings, and later he will entertain the company with songs, serious and comic. He had ambitions to be a first-class swimmer. He is the perfect Edwardian 'card'. How different from the withdrawn, aloof Stephen Dedalus. Thus, we can draw a distinction between Joyce as he was and as he created himself in his two novels.

It was because he partook of Dublin life in this varied way that Joyce was later able to describe it in minute detail in his work. He knew his Dublin, the genteel drawing-rooms, the prostitutes' kitchens, the world of chancers, ponces, bookies, boxers, jockeys, the milieu of literary Dublin, of professional Dublin.

This approach had its dangers. He could have become over-involved. He might have turned into a Dublin 'character'. The city in Joyce's time had plenty of these. Of inexhaustable resource in argument, or in the organisation of escapades, they siphoned off, into the creation of their personality, energy which might have been used to better purpose. Joyce's friend, John Elwood, (Temple in *A Portrait of the Artist as a Young Man*) had a name for them; they were 'artists', those who created their characters for the diversion of their friends. Joyce recognised the futility of such a course. When he had gathered his swag he cleared out.

There were many frustrations inherent in Irish life at that time for young men of Joyce's class. He belonged to the Catholic middle-class. William Fallon has given a good description of their dilemma in his essay. Regarded by their rulers as a subject race, they had a built-in sense of insecurity. The Church ruled them with a firm hand. It was not an atmosphere in which the individual could flourish without prolonged effort. Joyce intended to reserve his energy for the only thing that counted in his life – his art. As well, there were weaknesses in his character which could have finished his career as a writer if he had been subjected to the pressures of Irish life at that time, when talent often aborted through lack of opportunity for men of his religion and class. Perhaps he sensed what the fate of some of his brilliant contemporaries would be; poor drunken Kettle, dying disillusioned on the Western Front; George Clancy, (Davin in *A Portrait of the Artist*) murdered by the Black and Tans when he was Lord Mayor of Limerick; Vincent Cosgrave, (Lynch in *A portrait of the Artist*) jumping off Westminster Bridge 1909. Joyce seems to have become somewhat of a drunkard in later life; he had developed a strong persecution mania. He was classic material for failure had he remained in Dublin. One can almost hear the conversation in one of the city pubs:

'Do yeh see your man over there with a few jars on him. Him with the gunner eye and the nutcracker chin?'

'Yes.'

'Well, he's a genius – a ravin' bloody genius. He's writin' a book, and when it comes out, will I tell you somethin'?'

'What.'

'Yeats and that crowd will be left standin'.'

But Joyce had no intention of becoming another pregnant writer celebrated by brilliant failures in his native town, which regarded promise more kindly than fulfillment. Exile was the answer... and his blotting-paper memory and a trunkful of notes ensured that he could leave Dublin and still have the material for literature. 'I never really left it. I carry it around with me,' he told a friend in 1937.

There is no doubt that he missed Dublin. Visitors from Dublin were bombarded with questions. W. G.

Fallon and Eugene Sheehy recall how Joyce cross-examined them in minute detail about the city they had just left. He even seems to have become at times militantly pro-Irish. To Padraic Colum he will admit no other saint but St. Patrick. To Arthur Power he argues that Irish culture has an advantage over France and Britain, because it was never submitted to Roman rule. To Judge Sheehy's sister he said, 'Dublin will be found on my heart when I die.'

But the irony is that some infirmity of will prevented him from returning there. Originally he had fled Dublin to become a writer. An ascetic streak, inherited perhaps from his early religious period, enabled him to persevere in exile, no matter how strong the lure of home was for him. But after he had published *Ulysses,* there was no reason why he should not have returned. In fact there were strong reasons why he should have. His father, for whom he had a deep affection, was in poor circumstances, (as Padraic Colum relates), and would have welcomed a visit from his famous son. Ireland had become free. The new State might be interesting to one who had left it in bondage. Above all, there was no danger that he might succumb to the congenial lure of the city. He had achieved his purpose. He could relax.

From the point of view of future work, if he was to continue to write about Dublin, how long could he afford to stay away from it? By staying away *too* long Joyce may have diminished the very gift which he went into exile to preserve. But he had become incapable of going back. He invented every excuse to avoid setting foot in Ireland.

He never returned. Did he instead turn in on himself? Some of the accounts given here suggest that there are sections of *Finnegans Wake* which are too personal to communicate on any level. William Fallon relates here how he discovered that Joyce inserted the names of international Irish Rugby players in *Finnegans Wake*. (He and Joyce had watched Ireland play France in Paris in the twenties.) Padraic Colum found the name of an unknown music-hall artiste whom he and Joyce had seen in Dublin, slipped into the book under the disguise of a clever pun. Was Joyce in the tradition of the early Irish monks, who cut themselves off from life, and fascinated by intricacy inscribed their illuminations, in cells of their own making.

There can be no doubt about his other work. *Ulysses* is the most remarkable prose work in English of our time. *Dubliners* contains the first short stories of their kind in English. *A Portrait of the Artist as a Young Man* has become a classic. Joyce is the rival in the English language to Proust and Thomas Mann in French and German.

This book is written by his friends. They grew up in a Golden Age, the age of the Irish Literary Revival. It was a remarkable period, the period of Yeats, Synge, A.E., Lady Gregory, James Stephens,

Oliver Gogarty, Padraic Colum, Sean O'Casey, as well as Joyce. We can catch something of its flavour in these pages.

It seems sad that Joyce was away from it all when he died in Zürich in 1941. Even had he wished to, the war would have prevented him from returning to Ireland. But he may not have been so far away after all. He could still carry Dublin around in his mind. They found the book he was reading on his desk after his death. It was the life of Ireland's patron saint, St. Patrick, by Oliver St. John Gogarty, Joyce's pal in his student years in Dublin.

Ulick O'Connor

Eugene Sheehy

James Augustine Joyce was his full name, but he soon dropped the middle name.

He was an intimate friend, both at school and college, of my brother, Richard and myself, and he came very often to my father's house in Belvedere Place and in the 'Feuilles de notre Manuscrites' displayed at the Joyce exhibition in Paris recently, there are several references to 'chez Sheehy' and to talks between Joyce and various members of my family.

As I remember him then, he was a tall slight stripling with flashing teeth – white as a hound's – pale blue eyes that sometimes had an icy look, and mobile sensitive mouth. He was fond of throwing back his head as he walked, and his mood alternated between cold, slightly haughty, aloofness and sudden boisterous merriment.

Sometimes his abrupt manner was a cloak for shyness. He refers in an early manuscript to 'the induration of the shield', meaning that each of us has to forge in self-protection a shield to interpose between oneself and the hostile world.

James Joyce came to Belvedere from Clongowes Wood College, and was in a class, one year ahead of me, for the Intermediate examinations. Joyce, the schoolboy, was aloof, icy and imperturbable. He took the same pleasure, too, in baiting his masters and the Rector that he afterwards revelled in at the expense of his university professors.

One day, when Father Henry was taking my class for Latin, Joyce was sent in by the English master, Mr. Dempsey, to report he had been late for school. The Rector delivered quite a long lecture to Joyce to which the latter listened in unrepentant silence. When the lecture had finished, Joyce added, as if by way of afterthought and in a very bored manner: 'Mr. Dempsey told me to tell you, Sir, that I was half an hour late also yesterday.' This led to a second telling-off, almost as long as the first, and when it had run its course, Joyce took up the running again – this time almost with a yawn:

'Mr. Dempsey told me to tell you, Sir, that I have not been in time for school any day this month.'

This method of confessing one's transgressions was calculated to break the heart of any headmaster, and I fear that at Belvedere Joyce added many grey hairs to Father Henry's head.

It was Father Henry whom Joyce burlesqued in the school play at Belvedere, so vividly described in his book – *Stephen Hero*. I was seated in the gallery of the school when the play was produced, and witnessed the performance. The Reverend Rector had many mannerisms and clichés. For instance, a common practice of his was to announce: 'Any boy who cannot confidently feel that he can answer the Roman History, stand up,' and then, after sizing up with a shrewd glance the boys whose eyes did not sparkle with too bright or confident a light, he would add the dire command: 'Up Sheehy, up Lenehan!' as the case might be.

Joyce, who was cast for the part of a schoolmaster in the school play, ignored the rôle allotted to him and impersonated Father Henry. He carried on, often for five minutes at a time, with the pet sayings of the Rector, imitating his gestures and mannerisms. The other members of the caste collapsed with laughter on the stage – completely missing their cues and forgetting their parts – and the schoolboy audience received the performance with hysterical glee.

Father Henry, who was sitting in one of the front rows, again showed what a sportsman he was by laughing loudly at this joke against himself and Joyce received no word of reprimand for his impudence.

In the gymnasium I remember Joyce was always good for a joke. We had a new gymnastic master one year. Joyce arrived in to class doubled up like a hunchback. 'I've come in to be cured' he told the sergeant, amid laughter from the other students. 'My stomach muscles are tight from hunger' he said on another occasion when I asked him how he could do interminable pumpswings on the parallel bars. He was skilled at turning poverty into a joke.

In the year 1899 when I was sixteen years old, I passed from school to university – from one Board of Examiners to another. The Royal University of

Ireland was more of an examining board than a university. A student could obtain a degree without attending any lectures.

The lectures which I had to attend were few, and afforded me ample time to browse elsewhere. The real Alma Mater at this time was the National Library in Kildare Street. We read for our examinations in the library upstairs, but there were rather prolonged adjournments to the steps outside, where we heard the views on art and life and literature of Joyce, Kettle, Skeffington, Arthur Clery, John Marcus O'Sullivan, William Dawson, Constantine Curran and many other well-read and cultured men. Meeting and conversing with such men was no mean substitute for the wisdom that emanates from the professorial chairs in other universities, and the debates in the Physics Theatre of the college in 86 St. Stephen's Green reached as high a standard during this period as they are ever likely to attain.

I remember, for instance, a great occasion on which James Joyce read a paper on *Drama and Life* for the Literary and Historical Society. He had previously submitted the script of his address to the Rev. President of the college for his approval. The latter, finding much to disagree with in Joyce's whole-hearted praise of Ibsen's plays, passed a blue pencil through some of the passages in the address. Joyce, however, refused to read his paper if these passages were deleted. He discussed the matter with the President and to enforce his argument even lent him copies of the plays for his perusal. The result was that Joyce carried the day and read his paper without a word omitted.

A strong opposition was, however, marshalled to criticize the views expressed therein. Dr. William Magennis, Arthur Clery, W. P. Coyne, Hugh Kennedy (the late Chief Justice) and others attacked Joyce very vehemently and from every angle. Joyce rose to reply at about 10 p.m. when the bell was ringing in the landing outside to signal that it was time to wind up the proceedings. Joyce spoke without a note for about forty minutes and dealt with each of his critics in turn. It was a masterly performance and delivered to the accompaniment of rounds of applause from the back benches, which quite drowned the noise of the futile curfew on the landing outside.

After the debate had finished Seamus Clandillon expressed the views of many when he clapped Joyce vigorously on the back and exclaimed: 'Joyce, that was magnificent, but you're raving mad!'

Joyce took his degree in the Royal University and I saw a good deal of him during his time in college. He treated both his lectures and examinations as a joke, and it is to the credit of the university and its professors that, in spite of all this, he passed through successfully. He told me, from time to time, how he enjoyed himself in the examination hall. He considered that the poet Cowper was only fit to write the rhymes which are found in the interiors of Christmas crackers. When requested, therefore, to write an appreciation of *The Task,* he finished off two pages of scathing disparagement of its author with an adaptation of Hamlet's farewell to the dead Polonius: 'Peace tedious old fool!' Addison was another bête noire: referring to his summons to Steele to 'See how a Christian can die', Joyce berated him as the world's greatest hypocrite, and lapsed into Chaucerian English to state that the great 'Atticus' himself 'helpen nightly to his litter'.

It was, however, at his oral examination in English for his B. A. degree that he excelled himself. One of the learned professors put to him the question: 'How is poetic justice exemplified in the play of *King Lear*?'

Joyce replied very briefly: 'I don't know.'

The examiner, who had full knowledge of Joyce's literary ability, was not satisfied with this reply. 'Oh come, Mr. Joyce, you are not doing yourself justice. I feel sure that you have read the play.'

'Oh yes!' replied Joyce, 'but I don't understand your question. The phrase 'poetic justice' is unmeaning jargon so far as I am concerned.'

Joyce and I both attended the same class for Italian. Our lecturer was an Italian Jesuit named Father Ghezzi, who had been in India for many years and spoke English perfectly. Joyce had a wonderful aptitude for foreign languages and spoke Italian like a native, though, at that time, he had never left Dublin. My function in the class was to listen to Father Ghezzi and Joyce discuss philosophy and literature in Italian; and, for all I could understand of the dialogue, I would have been more profitably engaged in taking high dives from the springboard at the Forty-foot Hole in Sandycove.

A close companion of Joyce at the college was George Clancy, who was afterwards Mayor of Limerick, and was shot by the 'Black and Tans'. Clancy was a well-built and dark-haired son of Munster who was keen on Gaelic games and the restoration of our ancient language. He had a keen sense of humour and no guile. The simplicity and sincerity of his character appealed to Joyce, and I suspect that the character described as Davin in *A Portrait* covers his identity.

He and Joyce, at French class, made merry at the expense of Professor Cadic. Joyce would snigger whilst Clancy was translating into English a passage from a French text-book. Clancy pretended to take offence, demanded an instant apology, which was refused, and thereupon challenged Joyce to a duel in the Phoenix Park. The professor intervened to prevent bloodshed; the performance ended with handshakes all round; and the guileless Frenchman never appreciated what a farce it all was. One day Joyce entered the class-room about twenty minutes late; and, ignoring the professor's presence, went over to one of the large front windows of No. 86, threw it up, and stuck his head out. Monsieur Cadic, by a counter stroke, in order to upset Joyce's equilibrium, went to the other window, threw it up, and putting his head well out, looked at the offending pupil. 'Bonjour, M'sieu!' said the imperturbable Joyce, 'I was counting the carriages in Alderman Kernan's funeral.'

John Byrne Francis, the 'Cranly' of Joyce's *A Portrait* was also a fellow-student of mine at the College. He was a very clever man, had read most of the best literature and was a brilliant conversationalist. He was also one of the best chess players in Ireland at this period.

Joyce and he carried on long conversations in Dog Latin, to which each contributed an ingenious quota. 'Ibo crix oppidum', for instance, signified: 'I am going across town': 'ad manum ballum jocabimus' – 'We will play handball'; and 'regnat felices atque canes' – 'it is raining cats and dogs'. And, in more correct Latin, another bright effort on the part of 'Cranly' resulted in the aphorism 'Nomina stultorum ubique scribuntur'. It may be that these talks were, on Joyce's part, the first intimation of the vocabulary of *Finnegan's Wake*.

Joyce could have been a great actor. Even in his late teens, he was keen on dramatics and took part in family theatricals. I remember him playing in Belvedere Place the part of the English Colonel in Robertson's *Caste*, and he played it to the life.

He acted also with my sister, Margaret, in the old X.L. Cafe in Grafton Street in a play written by her, called *Cupid's Confidante*, in which he played the part of the villain – Geoffrey Fortescue.

In charades in our house on Sunday nights he was the star turn. His wit and gift for improvisation came into ready play. He was also a clever mimic and his impassive poker face helped his impersonations.

I remember on one occasion a burlesque of *Hamlet* performed by him and William Fallon. Joyce played the Queen Mother to Fallon's Ophelia, and the performance would rival that of Jimmy O'Dea at his best. As Ophelia, with appropriate comments, laid on the carpet some pieces of carrot and onion – the best substitutes for yew and rosemary – Hamlet's mother (who bore a striking resemblance to 'Mrs. Mulligan of the Coombe'), performed all the motions of a woman 'keening' at an Irish wake in the very ecstasy of grief.

Joyce had a beautiful tenor voice, and one of his earliest ambitions was to be a singer. His mother sometimes came to our house and played on the piano the accompaniments to his songs. I remember her as a frail, sad-faced, and gentle lady whose skill at music suggested a sensitive, artistic temperament. She was very proud and fond of Joyce, and he worshipped her. I can still see him linking her towards the piano, with a grave Old World courtesy. When she was not present, he played by ear his own accompaniments.

He had a wide range of ballads, English and Irish.

His favourite songs were *Take a Pair of Sparkling Eyes* from *The Gondoliers*; and the Serenade by Shelley beginning 'I arise from dreams of thee'.

He revelled, however, with a zest worthy of Falstaff in such rousing ballads as *Blarney Castle*, *Bold Turpin Hero*, and *When McCarthy Took the Flure at Enniscorthy*.

Another 'flash-back' to Belvedere Place reveals him, with cane, hat and eyeglass, swaggering up and down the room in the manner of Charles Coburn, as he sang with gusto *The Man Who Broke the Bank at Monte Carlo*.

He also sang a half-comic, half-plaintive Irish love song which I have heard from no other lips.

I heard him sing this ballad so often that I still remember every word of it. It contained two verses as follows:

'Oh Molly, I can't say you're honest,
Sure you've stolen the heart from my breast,
I feel like a bird that's astonished
When the young vagabonds steal its nest;
So I'll throw up a stone at the window,
And in case any glass I should break,

It's for you all the panes that I'm taking,
Yerra! what wouldn't I smash for your sake.

They say that your Father is stingy,
And likewise that your Mother's the same,
So it's mighty small change that you'll bring me
Excepting the change of your name.
So be quick with that change dearest Molly,
Be the same more or less, as it may,
And my own name, my Darling, I'll give you
The moment that you name the day.'

At the end of each verse he sang the following refrain
which was, to say the least of it, unusual:

'Ochone! Pillaloo! Och I'm kilt!
May the quilt.
Lay light on your delicate form,
When the weather is hot
But my love, when 'tis not,
May it cradle you cosy and warm.
Nic nurum ni roo!
Nic Nurum ni!'

Some of his humorous items he undoubtedly picked
up from his father who, I understand, had in his day
quite a reputation as a singer of comic songs in the
concert halls of County Cork.

The song commencing: 'Tis youth and folly makes

young men marry', which Joyce heard his father singing in the Victoria Hotel, Cork, as described in *A Portrait,* was also a favourite of the son and I often heard him sing it. He sang these old favourite ballads of his father, too, with 'the quaint accent and phrasing' to which Joyce refers in his book. According to Joyce Senior, no one could sing an Irish ballad like Mike Lacy.

'He had little turns for it, grace notes that he used to put in that I haven't got.'

I suspect that he was too modest in this disclaimer, for his son sang these old songs with quaint phrasing and grace notes that must have been in the full Lacy tradition.

His father was a dapper little man, with military moustache, who sported an eyeglass and cane, and wore spats, and I can quite believe that on the stage he could do *George Lashwood* to the life.

I would say, too, that James owed his rather caustic wit to his male parent. I remember Joyce relating to me one sample.

His father, at breakfast one morning, read from the Freeman's Journal, the obituary notice of a dear friend, Mrs. Cassidy.

Mrs. Joyce was very shocked and cried out: 'Oh! Don't tell me that Mrs. Cassidy is dead.'

'Well, I don't quite know about that,' replied her husband, 'but someone has taken the liberty of burying her.'

26

After his retirement from the rates office, Joyce Senior apparently devoted a good deal of his spare time to studying the pictures in *Tit Bits* and *Answers* which gave the clues to the names of railway stations – substantial prizes being offered each week to those competitors who were most successful in naming the stations depicted.

Joyce appeared to be entertained by this hobby of the old man. He told me that in the form he filled up, when seeking admission to the university, he described his father's occupation as 'going in for competitions'.

Joyce had legends for some of the Dublin statues. Of that of Bishop Plunket in Kildare Place, who has a finger thoughtfully on his brow, he said that the pose suggested: 'Now, where on earth did I put that stud?' And the statue of the poet Moore in College Green supplied with right forefinger raised the satisfied answer: 'Oh! I know.'

Of the numerous lampoons and limericks which he wrote at this time, I can recall one on Lady Gregory:

'There was an old lady named Gregory,
Who cried: 'Come all poets in beggary'.
But she found her imprudence,
When hundreds of students
Cried: 'We're in that noble category'.'

I recall also Joyce and his friend, Oliver Gogarty, engaging in a Limerick competition. Gogarty would have been the complete reincarnation of an 18th century 'Buck' if he hadn't been a fine poet as well. We didn't know much about his poetry at that time, but we knew him as an athlete, swimmer and author of wild verse. He was a student at Trinity College and dressed with great dash. I remember well his alert elegant bearing. He was on terms with every section of the community from the Ascendancy to the 'characters' of the back streets. Someone had challenged Joyce and Gogarty to compose Limericks on extempore subjects; they took up the challenge. The first subject was Yeats' visit to the United States on a lecture tour. The second was Dr. O'Dwyer, Bishop of Limerick, who had recently been engaged in a controversy with a Trinity Don concerning the height of the spire of the new Church he was building. I can't for the life of me remember accurately which Limerick was written by whom, but I rather imagine the first one was Gogarty's

A theatrical tenebris Yeats,
Went out on a tour to the States,
He preached against pelf, but he collared himself,
About 50 per cent of the gates.

To him answered Dr. O'Dwyer,
How dare you disparage our spire,

You protestant liar, just to defy you,
We'll build it fifty times higher.

I have already mentioned that it took a good deal to disturb Joyce's equanimity. On one occasion my brother and I were walking together in Phibsborough Road. We saw Joyce approaching us waving aloft what seemed to be a small Venetian blind. He was followed, at some paces interval, by his brother Stanislaus, who appeared to be hugely amused at James' antics. Joyce was very excited.

'Look what I have here,' he said. 'This is an Indian poem written in Sanskrit on ribbed grass, and I am going to sell it to the Professor of Languages in Trinity College.'

He opened up the book to show us the ribbed grass and the writing thereon. When he had the lattice work open in full length, a nursery maid in charge of a perambulator, whose attention at the moment was evidently not on her job, drove into him from behind with the result that he fell back into the carriage of the pram. Joyce was not the least bit perturbed. Still holding the book wide open on his lap, he half turned to the nurse and said very calmly: 'Are you going far, Miss?'

Joyce had an impish humour. He did the most whimsical things, often to his own detriment. Once, when paid to sing at a Dublin concert, he walked off the stage because he did not like the accompaniment; the fee, which he forfeited, meant a small fortune to him at the time. On another occasion, he went to London to meet William Archer, the critic, who was much impressed by Joyce's contribution to the *Fortnightly Review* on Ibsen's play *When We Dead Awaken*; Archer introduced Joyce to the editor of a literary magazine, who gave him a book of poems to review. Joyce castigated the unfortunate poet in merciless fashion. This did not please the editor.

'This will not do, Mr. Joyce,' he said.

'Sorry!' said Joyce, and proceeded to leave the room.

It was characteristic of him that he would never condescend to argue any point.

'Oh! come Mr. Joyce,' pleaded the editor, 'I am only anxious to help you. Why won't you meet my wishes?'

'I thought,' replied Joyce, 'that I was to convey to your readers what I considered to be the aesthetic value of the book you gave me.'

'Precisely,' said the editor, 'that is what I want.'

'Well!' replied Joyce, 'I don't think it has any value whatsoever, aesthetic or otherwise, and I have tried to convey that to your readers, and I presume that you have readers.'

This remark naturally nettled the editor, and he said: 'Oh! well, Mr. Joyce, if that is your attitude, I can't help you. I have only to lift the window and put my head out, and I can get a hundred critics to review it.'

'Review what?' said Joyce, 'your head?' and this ended the interview.

This incident is, of course, 'ex relatione' Joyce, but I believe that it happened, as he was, in my opinion, a very truthful man.

He also loved to challenge others to do whimsical acts. One night I heard him wager Skeffington half a crown, that the latter would not purchase one half-penny worth of gooseberries in the most expensive fruit shop in O'Connell Street and tender a golden sovereign in payment.

Skeffington took the bet and gave his miserly order to the lady shop assistant. When he offered the sovereign in payment, the lady said in rather frigid tone:

'Could you not make it something more, sir?'

'No,' replied Skeffington, 'I can't afford it,' and he collected his gooseberries and his change.

Joyce had witnessed all this from the door of the shop and whooped with glee at the performance.

The year after John McCormack won the Gold Medal for tenor singing at the Annual Feis Ceoil in Dublin, Joyce was a candidate for the same competition. Joyce would have secured the Gold Medal if he had attempted the sight reading test, but his 'integrity' would not permit, and he was disqualified.

It is worthy of note in this connection, that a

friend of mine, Mr. William Reidy, the Dublin cellist, has an old programme of a concert in the Antient Concert Rooms, in which the name of James Joyce would appear to have pride of place over that of John McCormack. The date of the concert is not mentioned. My guess is that it took place in the year 1902.

After Joyce left Dublin, I lost touch with him for some years, though he wrote to my father on the death of my brother Richard, and at another time sent me an Italian newspaper in which he had written an article – *Il Fenianismo* – on the death of John O'Leary, the great Fenian leader, who, by the way, presided at one of the debates in the Literary and Historical Debating Society when I was in the College.

One night in the year 1909 during a production by the Abbey Theatre of Shaw's *Blanco Posnet* I met Joyce again. He tapped me on the shoulder from behind with his walking stick, and then greeted me nonchalantly, as if we had met the previous day. He told me that he had come to Dublin to do the critique of the play – which had been censored in Great Britain – for an Italian newspaper, *'Il Piccolo Sera'*. He also said that I would hear interesting news of him within the next few weeks. This had reference, I understand, to the fact that he was to be the manager of the first cinema in Dublin, the 'Volta' in Mary Street. I believe he did obtain the position, but, if so, he held it only for a very short period.

Joyce was very sparing in his praise of other writers; and I was surprised, therefore, when, on this occasion, he told me that he admired the works of George Meredith, and that he regarded *The Tragic Comedians* as a novel of outstanding merit.

Except for Ibsen and Dante, the only other author whom he favoured was James Clarence Mangan; and I remember the intense pleasure with which all those assembled one night in my father's house heard him recite *The Nameless One* by the hapless Irish poet.

The next and last time I met Joyce was in his flat in Paris in the year 1928, when he had become world famous. I found out his address in the Rue de Grenelle from Miss Sylvia Beech who, I understand, financed the publication of the first edition of *Ulysses* and whose book shop in Paris had on display on its shelves many photographs of Joyce.

She was charmed when I told her that I was an old school-companion of his, and she produced a photograph of a group of students and professors taken at University College. The photo had been taken by my friend, Con Curran, and the group included Joyce, and she was so pleased that I was able to name all the others, that she presented me with a free copy of *Transition*, in which Joyce's *A Work in Progress* was then being published. I regret to say that I never read the instalment in *Transition* as the first paragraph thereof convinced me that my un-tutored mind was not adequate to understand and appreciate Joyce's new 'vocabulary', as he himself termed it.

Later that day my wife and I called on Joyce at his flat, and met there, also his wife, son and daughter. Everything in Joyce's rooms spelt 'Dublin'. There were pictures and sketches of old Dublin on the walls, and even the design of the large rug, with which the floor was carpeted, portrayed the cork-screw course of the River Liffey.

He was delighted to meet me again, and his queries were all concerning the Dublin that he knew and loved.

'Where were now Tom and Dick and Harry?' naming former companions that I had well-nigh forgotten, and he became quite impatient that I could not call to mind at once one Jack O'Reilly, who had faded from the Dublin scene for many years.

'And how does Sallynoggin look now?' and 'the shops along the chief streets?'

And then he questioned me about some of Dublin's well known characters. For instance: 'Did J. B. Hall' – a reporter for the *Freeman's Journal* – 'still go round in all weathers with his overcoat slung over one shoulder?'

He was thrilled to know that the statue of Smith O'Brien had been moved from O'Connell Bridge, and was now lined up with the other statues in

O'Connell Street.

'Why was nobody told me that before?' he said rather petulantly.

My sister, Mrs. Sheehy Skeffington, told me that at a later date she had another such interview with Joyce. Half-dazed with his cascade of queries, she at length said to him:

'Mr. Joyce, you pretend to be a cosmopolitan, but how is it that all your thoughts are about Dublin, and almost everything that you have written deals with it and its inhabitants?'

'Mrs. Skeffington!' he replied, with a rather whimsical smile, 'There was an English queen who said that when she died the world 'Calais' would be written on her heart. 'Dublin' will be found on mine.'

Eugene Sheehy

William G. Fallon

What does one know of Victorian Dublin who only our sprawling modern capital knows? Upwards of seventy years ago Dublin was the decaying metropolis of a neglected Crown Colony with an Ascendancy in control of the public services and major business establishments. Waste and decline had long before set in commercially and socially in the wake of a Statute (1801), the effect of which was to unite the two Legislative Assemblies of Great Britain and Ireland. Thereafter and throughout the century the opulent families abandoned their town houses and withdrew to England if not to their landed estates in the Irish provinces. Save that the homes overlooking or adjacent to Dublin's squares held on somehow, it was inevitable that the spacious buildings flanked as they were by unique avenues of Georgian domestic architecture would in time degenerate into dilapidated tenements. So it came to pass, and the City's Corporation despaired of finding a solution for the problem. This was *James Joyce's Dublin*. To fill the vacuum left by the streaming exodus of the Ascendancy and its entourage numerous families of the upper middle classes, availing of the tempo, awakened to the possibilities of improving their modest commercial activities or furtively edged their way into the professions. Daniel O'Connell's Catholic Relief Act and his Municipal Reform Association had, however, inadvertently provided those families with an additional incentive; that of social advancement; they duly proceeded to rectify their social deficiencies by means of suitable introductions to the Viceroy. The successful entrees were thereafter labelled 'Castle Catholics'. Contra, the generality of Dubliners, the bourgeoisie, bereft of outlets, were immobilised, anonymous, but passed muster as genteel. To Joyce, they were 'the obtuse middle class' and reconciled to their lot as if waiting until time shall be no more. Below was the unorganised welter of wage-earners in their crumbling dwellings. At times a veneer of colour relieved the depressing panorama, whenever, at routine parades, uniformed recruiting officers for the Royal Dublin Fusiliers canvassed the streets, or handwaves of greeting, coupled with amusement were extended to seasonal trippers from the Isle of Man who, nervously clutching the handrails of jaunting cars, were en route for Guinness's Brewery, the site of the assassination in the Phoenix Park of Burke and Cavendish in 1882, and therefrom to the National Museum. But the mean streets multiplied with the decades and slumdom had long prior been reckoned in terms of acres. We of the eldest generation retain memories of it all. *So, too, in his day, did Joyce.* To him it was 'the centre of paralysis'.

James Joyce was born in a southern suburb of Dublin and was sent to Clongowes Wood College at the age of five where he remained until 1891. Clongowes was a Jesuit institution. After an interval he arrived at Belvedere College in Dublin. This was a day-school also run by the Jesuits. He was then 11 years old. I had commenced there some time ahead of him. We youngest pupils used to be shepherded from the classrooms of the grownups and classified in groups according to age. Among other newcomers was an English-speaking Italian boy of about Joyce's own age. Both were allotted to our own particular group, although we were entering on our second year at the college. Joyce, as one might have expected, did not join in the preliminary boyish din; instead, he exchanged whispers with the Italian boy, whom he had previously met somewhere. Was this the beginning of his interest in Italy which he cultivated so assiduously in later years? He was also to remember later with affection the Jesuit scholastic who had charge of us that day, Mr. McArdle, S.J.

After a period at Belvedere, Joyce graduated to the Upper House. He won an Exhibition (scholarship) in junior and middle grade. He would perhaps have done even better in the examinations had it not been for his wide reading outside the prescribed course. One of our class-mates, Albrecht Connolly, used to tell us that Joyce could be seen every Saturday scouring the bookstalls for new works. Stannie (Jim's brother) used to say that Jim was always ahead of his homework, so much so that it left him time for all sorts of extra curricular reading, including opera scores.

Our English teacher was Mr. George Dempsey. Joyce always maintained that he owed Mr. Dempsey a debt for the way he had been taught English. Mr. Dempsey was the reader for a Dublin publisher and occasionally for a Catholic firm in London. The subjects he prescribed usually provided scope for any of us with imagination. Joyce availed of his liberality. On one occasion we had Lamb's Shakespearean Tales, an elementary text-book. Joyce instead handed in a composition on the essays of Elia. I remember, too, that after we had made some progress in Pope's *Essay on Man* in class, our task was to comment on the lines:

'Honour and shame from no condition rise;
Act well your part, there all the honour lies.'

'And Joyce,' Mr. Dempsey added, 'you may write whatever you like.' Yes; Joyce elected to write on Pope's translation of the *Odyssey*. Absit omen! He was no more than sixteen years old at the time. Connolly suggested that he must have picked it up at one of the second-hand bookstalls. This was his first introduction perhaps to the famous tale of which he was later to give his own twentieth century rendering. Another time Mr. Dempsey doubtless had a good and sufficient reason for turning to Joyce with – 'I am keeping yours,' when Jim, instead of a Shakespearean play prescribed by the Intermediate Education Board – submitted *Ibsen, Dramatist*. Joyce told me that it was through Mr. Dempsey he had made contact with the distinguished editor of *Fortnightly Review*, W. T. Stead, and subsequently contributed to that review his well known article on Ibsen's play, *When We Dead Awaken*.

Father William Henry, S.J., was Rector during those years. He was the last of the stern Victorian age at Belvedere. Early on he had systematically sought to probe into Joyce's puzzling equanimity with 'Proud boy, Joyce?' The reaction invariably was a respectful but granitic – 'No, Sir.' But no sooner had the victim been promoted to the Middle Grade than an unexpected relationship developed. The Rector was our principal teacher and in class Joyce, to his surprise, was all but word-perfect whether the subject was Fander's Catechism of Christian Doctrine, the Classics, or the History of Greece and Rome. What then? Mr. Dempsey, went periodically to Father Henry's office at the luncheon interval. Now Joyce was added to the Rector's table. What transpired there was not for us to hear; Joyce's lips were sealed. But a boy called Cassidy discovered what was afoot. He went one day on an errand to the Rector's room during lunch. He came back with the news: 'Joyce is getting a free lunch.' It seems that the Rector, knowing of the straitened circumstances of the Joyce family, and appreciating the talent of the young scholar, had seen to it, in the most tactful

43

way possible, that he was properly fed. There were three disconnected sequels to this event. Joyce became head of the Senior Sodality, he joined the recently established gymnastic class in the college theatre, and Mr. Dempsey gave increasing attention to his weekly essays. As Prefect of the school Sodality, Joyce with the others would go to Confession and Holy Communion each month in the school chapel. This continued throughout the years he was at Belvedere. One has a clear recollection of this, because Joyce, being the Prefect, used to be the first to get up and lead the others out of chapel on Sodality mornings.

Joyce's antics in the gymnastic class could be most amusing. Light, slim and flexible as he was, he lacked the co-ordination for games, but he enjoyed the fun and companionship of other boys; that is what counted for him. I remember well his antics on the horizontal bar. There would be a call for help from the other side of the gymnasium. We would look over and see Jim's lanky figure entangled, that is the only word I can use, on the horizontal bar. His legs were where his feet should be and vice versa. Jim's call would be a sort of a screech, a brief but penetrating cackle of laughter. When we would disentangle him and get him down he would relapse into sudden silence and become desperately solemn. This sudden change from laughter to solemnity was a particular characteristic of his. He came to football matches with us in the Phoenix Park. Fr. Thomkin, our Prefect of Studies, used to bring us out there. Joyce would give up playing after a while and slide off to the touch line, but he never went away. He always stayed on to watch. He wasn't able to kick the ball properly, for some reason. He would kick it with his heel like a girl. When we set out for home, there Joyce would be in the van, but striding out alone.

He was a good walker. I would always go by tram to the Bull Wall to swim, Joyce would walk there and back (about 4 miles). It may surprise many to know that he was an expert swimmer. He was accomplished not only at the breast stroke, but the trudge as well. This was due in a measure to his lean frame and lithe build, but mainly to his determination in practice. At the Bull Wall where free bathing facilities were provided, he had become friendly with a fellow swimmer, Dr. Vincent O'Brien. Vincent O'Brien was John McCormack's singing teacher, and was the first, I believe, to make Joyce's fine singing voice known to the public. Joyce admired Vincent's swimming ability. O'Brien used to swim out from the Bull Wall towards the Liffey, a risky swim for anyone but a strong swimmer. Joyce confided to me that he hoped some time to emulate his hero and brave the Liffey currents. He would often strike amusing poses when he was in swimming togs. I remember one day out at the Bull Wall when the sky was leaden and the sea extremely rough. When I arrived at our bathing place, Joyce was sitting on a rock shivering. He was just out of the water and had not even dried his hair. 'What on earth do you represent now?' I asked. 'Hunger,' he replied, without a smile. Was this the 'induration of the shield'?

I remember on another occasion he came to his first swimming lesson in Tara Street Baths. He had borrowed a clumsy safety outfit from a Ringsend seaman. But, on entering the shallow water, his head and shoulders went under, and his feet rose above the surface as a result of misadjusting the contraption. As soon as he regained the perpendicular, a sudden gale of laughter, a prolonged cackle, greeted his onlookers, followed immediately by silence and a fixed gaze as if looking through us to a distant object beyond.

Joyce asked me to propose him for my own swimming club, Pembroke. If he had become a member, he would have competed in swimming races, but he had left Dublin before I had an opportunity to propose him.

Albrecht Connolly, Joyce and I, used to find ourselves frequently in each other's company when we were at Belvedere. Connolly lived very near the College, and Joyce and I were within a short distance of it as well. I remember one occasion when we were all small boys, in the region of 13 years or so, Connolly, Joyce and I were walking home. Connolly asked Joyce to admit that Shakespeare was the greatest poet. Joyce would not do so. Connolly then twisted Joyce's arm, and continued to frog-march Joyce along beside him for quite a long period. As we were going in a different direction from Joyce's home, he knew that he would be late for tea. (Albie had a tendency to be a bully.) I have no idea whether Joyce thought that Shakespeare was the greatest English writer, or whether he had another choice of his own, but it was quite clear, one way or another, that he was not going to have criticism forced on him. He was in tears at Connolly's action, but he refused to yield. And he hadn't given in when Connolly released him after they had reached Connolly's home and he had to go in.

Companions of this period, sometimes went into Joyce's books under another name. Joyce used to play Red Indians with a family called Wilkins. These became Dillon when he used his recollection of the family as background in his story *Encounter* in *The Dubliners*.

Araby is one of the most poignant stories in *Dubliners*. It tells of a young boy going to a bazaar to buy a present for a favoured girl. But his uncle waits so long to give him the money that the boy arrives too late at the bazaar to buy the present he had marked out for his girl-friend. Strangely enough, I remember meeting Joyce on the very evening that he went to this bazaar. It *was* called *Araby*. I had just got off the train at Lansdowne Road when I spied him. The train used to draw in on the main line and then go into a siding to let off visitors to the bazaar. It was a Saturday night. When we reached the bazaar it was just clearing up. It was very late. I lost Joyce in the crowd, but I could see he was disheartened over something. I recall, too, that Joyce had had some difficulty for a week or so previously in extracting the money for the bazaar from his parent.

I believe that Joyce was a little too distant to be a close friend. When he was with us he sometimes appeared to be peering into the future. But he always entered into the spirit of things. One of the most notable things about him at school was his flair for observation linked to an uncanny memory. Incidents, not even of passing interest – a house that seemed to be unrelated to its fellows alongside, boys playing at marbles at the kerbstone of a roadway, a clump of dwarf trees, a distant view of a chimney stack of a brewery suddenly swinging into sight at a particular bend in an avenue, were all imprinted on his mind with photographic accuracy.

I think it appropriate to mention here a few observations of what I knew of Joyce's religious attitude as a schoolboy and a student. Stanislaus Joyce has recorded in his *Dublin Diary* of August 1904, that 'Jim had ceased to believe in Catholicism for many years'. This to my mind is an unjustifiable conclusion. It shows an inability to distinguish between commonplace irreverence or negligence and dogmatic disbelief.

I remember very well at University College that Jim continued to attend to his religious duties. He was a member of the College Sodality. This included going to Confession and Communion. He was also a member of St. Thomas Aquinas Academy. His sister, Sister Gertrude, who had become a nun in New Zealand, corresponded with me until her death in March 1964. She had exchanged letters with her brother, Jim, until his death in 1941. She prayed constantly for him during his lifetime and after his death.

I often think that Joyce would have been attracted to Teilhard de Chardin's interpretation of Catholicism, Joyce with his H.C.E. (Here Comes Everyman) who revolves in four cycles of human evolution. Perhaps Joyce got only half-way there. Teilhard's notion that man is progressing, that science and astronomy all converge on the infinite would, I believe, have greatly appealed to that side of Joyce's character which I feel was spiritual.

It must have been a refreshing experience for Joyce when he joined the old University College at St. Stephen's Green at that time under the Deanship of Fr. William Delaney, S.J. Although joining, he had no set purpose in seeking a university degree. Seemingly, Dublin University with its single college and classical façade could equally well have provided for his wayward requirements. But no! and not precisely because it happened to be a Protestant institution, but because of what to him was 'the otherness' of the place. He was the complete Dubliner. In Trinity he would have been a misfit. It is more likely, however, that his peevish comment as he found it at the turn of the century was that the only affluent college in the land had failed to live up to its former reputation in the sphere of letters and the fine arts. No doubt disciples of Antisthenes could always silence criticism by pointing to 'Trinity's' achievements on the cricket field and as the appointed Guardian Angel of the Book of Kells! It could have been that way with Joyce whenever he glanced at the statues of Goldsmith and Burke on his way to No. 86 St. Stephen's Green. At University College, at least, he would realise how native traditions and culture, held in common, were the bonds that linked his Dublin with the provinces. That revelation was Joyce's simple conception of Irish nationalism, but in the awakening political enthusiasm of those years he was wholly disinterested!* He graduated in 1902 at twenty years of age, modern languages being his forte. His attendance at lectures had been irregular, probably because, unlike a majority of the student body who had programmed their futures, Joyce had no plans, although he toyed for a while with the Col-

* But Joyce later took a keen interest in Arthur Griffith's Sinn Fein and thought it the only political group likely to succeed – Editor's note.

lege's Cecilia St. Medical School. Later on, still perplexed by his own indecision and hesitancy, Joyce availed of opportunities to meet Professor William Magennis and during the succeeding years they frequently conversed in the precincts of the College or following a meeting of the Literary and Historical Society. The Professor was 'student-minded' and used to encourage newcomers to join the Society and graduates to continue their membership. He lectured in the faculty of Mental Science and, as I knew, advised Joyce to read Cardinal Newman's autobiographic *Apologia Pro Vita Sua*. Actually, Joyce had passed unnoticed at the college until he began to take an active part in the Literary and Historical Society's debates. In those years, say 1899/1906, the fifty-five-year-old society overflowed with a membership of all the talents, its golden age, such as, according to seniority – Kent, Kennedy, MacGarry, Sheehy-Skeffington, (Joyce's 'McCann'), A. Clery, Patrick Pearse (of 1916 fame), Kettle, Walsh, O'Sullivan, Hackett, Curran, Kinahan (Moynihan in *The Portrait*), the brothers R. and E. Sheehy, G. Clancy ('Davin'), Rory O'Connor (of 'the Civil War'), to name a few without derogation of others, many of whom in the after years became notable personalities in their respective spheres of activity. Joyce would supplement any such list following his Ibsenesque address on *Drama and Life*. Another outstanding contribution was his *Clarence Mangan*,

51

with its individualistic analysis of that half-forgotten Irish poet. Yet the most attractive in the galaxy was not Joyce, but Kettle who crossed swords with Joyce in a well-remembered controversy on the ultra Celticism of Yeats' play *The Countess Cathleen*. It provoked Joyce's pamphlet *The Day of the Rabblement* which he published in conjunction with Frank Sheehy-Skeffington.

Commentators have afforded only minimal space to the influence J. F. Byrne ('Cranly' in *A Portrait*) imperceptibly exerted on Joyce's development. They had been at Belvedere College together and during their brief spells at the Medical School. (To us he was 'Jeffbyrne'.) Yet they were opposites, physically and intellectually; for as well as being a keen athlete Byrne's reading hours apparently ranged in compartments over the circle of human knowledge, the perfect encyclopedist in miniature. Parading the four sides of St. Stephen's Green, or Mountjoy Square, at times long after nightfall, I, on more than one occasion, 'listened in' to 'Jeffbyrne'. His deliberate procedure was, not to monopolise, but to provide what he facetiously termed 'Platonics'. But Joyce seemed to prefer Byrne, unaccompanied, for those leisurely walks. We have since learned that in those years, 1902–1904, Joyce had commended to outline a lay-out for his works of art and the Dublinised types he should select. To that end, who better than 'Jeffbyrne' who knew the Metropolis and its purlieus and sheebeens through-and-through and where Joyce could make personal contacts with his human material? Byrne was his trustworthy keeper.

I was to meet my friend Joyce in years later in unusual circumstances. In the twenties I was in Paris to watch Ireland playing France in a Rugby International. I rang Joyce and he asked me to come over to his flat. He seemed delighted to hear from me. When I arrived at the flat I discovered to my astonishment that he had been to see the match. 'How did you come to see the game, Joyce,' I said. 'I had to go and see the boys in green jerseys,' was his reply. Later I was to find that this visit to the Stades Columbes had not been wasted. Some time after my conversation with him, when I had returned to Dublin, I received a copy of *Transition* which had been despatched to me by Joyce. It was dated Summer 1928. It contained excerpts from the book he was currently writing, which was later to be published as *Finnegans Wake*. I was puzzled to know why Joyce had sent it. I read it carefully though I found it difficult to decipher. It seemed a new language. Then my eye caught the phrase: 'By the horn of twenty of both the saint Collopys blackmail him I will.' Could the 'saint Collopys' be the Collopy brothers who had played for Ireland in the International rugby match Joyce and I attended? My conviction that they were, increased as I found five further references to rugby in my copy of *Transition*. (The Collopy brothers, by the way, were anything but 'saints' on the rugby field.) 'In that united I.R.U. stade' obviously referred to the Irish Rugby Football Union and the Stade Columbes. 'And I'll tell you the Bective's wouldn't hold me' was a reference to my own rugby club, Bective Rangers. (Joyce would have known this club well. In his day the first XV contained seven or eight Old Belvederians, and he used to go out to the R.D.S. ground in Ballsbridge to watch Bective play.) 'I'd followed through my upfielded newviewscope the rugaby moon cumuliouly godrolling himself westasleep amuckst the cloudscrums' made use of a number of rugby metaphors; the moon seen as an oval ball in the scrum of the clouds. Another passage which contained metaphors from the rugby game was, 'Slip your oval out of touch and let the paravis be your goal. Up leather Prunella convert your try.' Certainly his visit to watch the 'boys in green jerseys' had not been wasted. These passages can be found on pages 457, 446, 451, 449, 435 in the Faber & Faber edition of *Finnegans Wake*.

In 1931, I was again over in Paris, but this time as an Irish selector. Joyce must have guessed I was in town for the match because he phoned me to come around and see him. He had two tickets for the match and was going accompanied by an enthusiast. I was unable to go with Joyce, but agreed to meet him later. When I got around to see him eventually that evening, having dodged the after-match dinner, he told me that his eyes had not been strong enough to identify 'our team'. He rolled off the names of the Irish players who had taken part in the game and their respective clubs. Then to my astonishment he talked of prominent players in the 1923 side and added that he had attended the alternate games played in the intervening seasons whenever he happened to be in Paris. A substantial part of our conversation was taken up talking about the match and the players. I noticed that he still spoke with a good class Dublin accent. When I told him something that amused him on this occasion, he would break off into that famous Ha! Ha! Ha! cackle of his that I remembered so well from the time when he was a schoolboy. He was preoccupied with memories of Dublin. He enquired about my former house in Fitzwilliam Street, and the College boys who lived in the same line of houses. Then he invited me to check the accuracy after naming and numbering the households on both sides of that residential Street in those far off years. He didn't overlook mention of a broad passageway that led to the residence and horse-training establishment of one Rogers, who, if we are to believe Joyce, wore 'leather leggins and a sports jacket day and night in mitigation of an iron-grey beard sprouting from a florid complexion'. (On my return to Dublin I checked Joyce's memory with the aide of a Thoms Dublin Directory, and found that he was correct in every item. At the same time I learned that the habit of listing a series of business names in shopping centres was one of Joyce's devises to retain pictures of his Dublin.)

'Do you remember,' he said, 'Fr. McArdle's catechism classes in 'The Little House'? Fr. McArdle rounded the benches and fastening on to the shortcomings of two boys, the Farrell's I think it was, and having been satisfied that I knew our penny catechism of Catholic Doctrine better than anyone else, dispatched all three of us to a corner of the room for me to take on the role of teacher.'

He talked about Albrecht Connolly, (this was the boy who had twisted Joyce's arm. In fact Joyce had been on much better terms with the Connollys than this incident would suggest) Albrecht was one of a talented family whose house was not far from Belvedere. He introduced Joyce to his widowed mother, brothers and sisters, and for a while Connolly's house was a second home for Joyce. I recall how I used to be puzzled why Mrs. Connolly would call Jim aside when we were all going home from school. We discovered later that she was taking Jim into the house to give him a meal. She knew of his difficult circumstances at home. One of Albrecht's sisters became a nun at the Loretto Convent. She had a clear recollection of Joyce, as I discovered when I visited her years later. She had been impressed by his imperturbability and precocious maturity as a young boy.

He had gone with Albrecht to visit her in the convent when he was in Dublin, and had also written to her from exile. She had taken a keen interest in his literary career and had followed the reviews of *Ulysses* and *Finnegans Wake* with avid interest. I bought her several of his early books including *Dubliners* and I remember the delight with which she received them.

Joyce's memory for detail on the occasion of my Paris visit was extraordinary. He recalled how he had exchanged whispers with the little Italian boy on his first day in Belvedere. He described our classroom with the crucifix over the fireplace, and listed, without hesitation, a score of the boy's names in our class; George Collins, Cassidy, Farrell, and others. We talked about the Wilkins boys with whom he had played Red Indians. Joe Wilkins, one of the boys, had later become a priest. Joyce seemed surprised at this. 'I never thought Joe would make a priest' was his comment.

He asked me to do 'Murphy'. By this he meant would I imitate our somewhat bucolic maths master at Belvedere. I impersonated for Joyce an incident when Murphy came into class looking somewhat the worse for the weather. Joyce had been sitting at the top of the class and said, 'You have a cold, sir?' Murphy muttered in his rich country voice, 'Thanks, that's only porter.' Joyce laughed at this, and I reminded him of the time I had played Ophelia to his

Queen mother in the charade at Sheehy's house. When he was told of Ophelia's fate, Joyce had replied in a thick Dublin accent, 'Ah, the poor gerrul' (girl). He recalled other evenings he had spent at the Sheehy home. He could remember the names and occupations of everybody who attended these soirées.

I reminded him of the time three of us had accompanied him on a walk on Sandymount Strand. He strode out in front of us. I quoted from 'Ulysses' and asked him was his description of the foul foreshore at Ringsend near the mouth of the Liffey taken from his experience on the walk that day:

'Unwholesome sand flats waited to such his threading soles breathing upwards sewage breath.'

He made no comment; but instead fixed me with his medusoid stare. Apropos of this, he remarked that during his school days he had experimented in storywriting about happenings with persons of interest to him, and brought a few of them to George Dempsey for his comments...

As tactfully as I could, I questioned Joyce about his eyesight. His only comment was an irritated 'Ah', a long-drawn-out sigh containing undertones of frustration.

We decided to share a taxi, and I would drop him off at the eye clinic. He was concerned about my safety in Paris at that time of night, though I had no great distance to go. That was the last time I was to see him.

I felt that with all the changes success and fame had wrought in him, James Joyce I had been talking to was not fundamentally different from the entertaining and brilliant companion I had known in our schooldays at Belvedere and later at University College.

William G. Fallon

Padraic Colum

When I first met James Joyce in 1901 or early in 1902, he was beginning to emerge as a Dublin 'character'. Already there was a legend about him.

That first meeting took place at one of Lady Gregory's evening parties. Seated in a corner were two young men whom I, who was about their age but had not been at the university, sized up as students. Now in Dublin at that time, students (they were mostly male) were thought of somewhat as they were in medieval times, as knowledgeable, profane, and, to a certain extent, detrimental. But these two were obviously not the ordinary run of students, since they were in a company (it would have been more fitting to say 'congregation') that included Lady Gregory and William Butler Yeats. Introduced to the two, I found I had heard their names before; they were Oliver Gogarty and James Joyce.

Each was already something of a celebrity. Oliver Gogarty, then a student at Trinity College, was known as an athlete – a bicyclist and a swimmer – as well as one to whom many of the scandalously witty sayings that were going the rounds of Dublin were attributed. The other's distinction was much less general. A year or two before that, when he was not much more than eighteen, James Joyce had achieved something that would have been gratifying to a writer twice his age; he had had an article published in the important *Fortnightly Review*. It was a review of Ibsen's *When We Dead Awaken,* for which the playwright, at that time the great master of European drama, later had William Archer, his English translator, express his appreciation to the young critic. It was a creditable article, one that showed erudition, loftiness of outlook, and, as one who read it thoughtfully could see, a dedication.

I do not remember that Joyce entered the conversation that evening. He and Gogarty sat apart, near the door, as if they did not quite belong at the gathering.

It may have been on this occasion that Lady Gregory asked Joyce to 'write something for our little theatre'. It was a request that the young author of *The Day of the Rabblement* was often to be derisive about. I don't know whether it was he or Gogarty who made up the limerick that is frequently quoted as Joyce's:

> There was a kind lady named Gregory,
> Who said: 'Come, all ye poets in beggary.'
> But she found her imprudence
> When hundreds of students
> Cried: 'We're in that ca-tegory.'

Several times after we were introduced at Lady Gregory's, Joyce and I came within recognizing distance on the street or in the National Library, but we had no communication. Joyce was aloof, and his blue eyes, perhaps because of defective vision, seemed intolerant of approach. He would enter the rotunda of the reading room generally between eight and nine o'clock in the evening. I won't say that he entered arrogantly, but he entered as one who was going to hold himself aloof from the collectivity there. Once, when I came to the counter after he had been there, an attendant said of a book that had been put aside, apparently to be reserved, 'For Mr. Joyce'. It was a book on heraldry.

Then, when Joyce and I were mentioned together as young poets, it was proper, I felt, that we should have some intimacy; this I decided one evening as we passed each other in the library. As he went through the turnstile on his way out, I went through too and spoke to him.

I think he took my approach as an act of homage (it was) and was willing to go along with me conversationally. We went out on Kildare Street and kept walking on, then along O'Connell Street until we turned toward where he lived. By this time Joyce was talking personally, or perhaps I should say biographically.

Looking back on that promenade, I know that I could have had no better introduction to the personality and the mind of that unique young man. He talked as a formed person talking to one whom he suspected of being unformed; he delivered, as he often did in those days, some set speeches. What maturity he had then!

It was natural to think, and I suppose I thought it, that a young man who distrusted, as he told me, all enthusiasms, was a singular character. And for Joyce to say this in the Dublin of the day was to set himself up as a heretic or a schismatic, and one who rifles the deposit of faith. I am trying to find a word for the way the young man standing on that street corner said, 'I distrust all enthusiasms'. It was not with any youthful bravado. It was rather like one giving a single veto after a tiring argument.

But it is not Joyce as the young man who separated himself from the rest of us, nor Joyce as the son of a Dublin personage, that I remember from that fortunate evening; rather it is Joyce as the maker of beautifully wrought poems. Joyce spoke his verse with deliberateness and precision, but in a naturally beautiful voice that had been cultivated for singing. The effect was more personal than in the case of AE or Yeats; it was Joyce exalted into the mode in which he knew himself free. 'The simple liberation of a rhythm'; this was his definition of the lyric at the time. I remember his rendering of lyrics that were favourites with him then – a rendering without the lilt that Irish poets are apt to give the verse they are repeating, one in which the poem became stylized speech (but with exceptional beauty of voice). I recall his reading of Ben Jonson's: *Still to be neat, still to be drest,* I remember, too, his rendering of Beatrice's song in the last act of *The Cenci*

– 'False friend, wilt thou smile or weep, When my life is laid asleep?' And a lyric of Mangan which even that poet's most devoted readers have passed over, became memorable when repeated by him: *Veil not thy miror, sweet Amine.'*

After this first talk with him, I did not see Joyce for some time. He left Dublin for Paris in the fall of 1902, stopping over in London to get some reviewing to do – the normal way for a young Dublin man of letters to cash in on his bookishness. Yeats was in London then and helped Joyce with introductions to editors.

He was away from Dublin for some months; then I heard that he had returned and later that his mother had died. I wrote a note of sympathy and received a formal acknowledgement. My family name has variant spellings, and when I wrote the note I used the one with the horrible 'b' at the end, a form that a grandparent quite mistakenly had used. The next time I saw Joyce he was standing despondently where there was a small company. In a distant way he said, 'I had a letter from you – or can it be there are two doves?' (In Latin, Irish, and French my name means that.) I mentioned the variations in spelling. 'And which do you use when your singing robes are about you?'

This was Joyce at his most detached. All of us used the cold approach from time to time, of course – the 'frozen mitt' was often proferred. Still, Joyce's attitude of ironic detachment toward me was not surprising. The nationalist group around *The United Irishman* with which I was associated, was to him nothing more than 'the rabblement'. AE, whose Hermeticism he despised, was promoting whatever stock I had. Perhaps Joyce thought of me then as one of those whom he later described as:

Those souls have not the strength that mine has
Steeled in the school of old Aquinas.

But he seemed to be kin, at this stage, with his own 'comedian Capuchin'. The gestures he made with the ashplant he now carried, his way of making his voice raucous, were surely part of an act. And wasn't there, too, in his behaviour, the assertion of a young man conscious of his hand-me-down clothes, whose resort was the pawn office, and who was familiar with the houses in Nighttown? The raucous voice, the obscene limericks delivered with such punctilio... Was he playing Rimbaud? Villon?

It appeared that Joyce had brought back from Paris a cabaret song, *Cadet Rousele,* and would sing it at certain gatherings. So Oliver Gogarty had that name for him too: 'Have you seen Cadet Rousele?' The name suited the figure that, yachting cap on his head, tennis shoes on his feet, ashplant in hand, per-ambulated the streets of Dublin: Cadet Rousele. It was as though there were two projections of Joyce in those days, one his own person and the other the comic persons with which Gogarty invested him.

It was solely as a 'character' and that partly a Gogartian creation, that Joyce was known to Dubliners of that time. To himself, of course, he was altogether different; he had none of the approachableness, privately, of a 'character':

That high, unconsortable one –
His love is his companion.

But since the early Ibsen article he had written nothing, beyond the Mangan essay and a few lyrics shown to friends, so far as anyone knew. That he was an intellectually exceptional young man anyone who met him could tell, but they also knew he had frequently been in the gutter. There had been other brilliant young Dubliners who were now but fading 'characters'. Needless to say, no one foresaw *Ulysses* or *Portrait of the Artist* or even *Dubliners*.

About that time an early play of mine was produced by the National Theatre Society. Joyce asked me to let him see the script. I did. Afterward I encountered him in O'Connell Street, and he treated me to a private 'performance'. Pointing his ashplant at me, he said, 'I do not know from which of them you derive the most misunderstanding – Ibsen or Maeterlinck.' He had the script with him: the encounter must have been planned. It was in a roll, which permitted him to make its presentation to me significant. 'Rotten from the foundation up,' he said.

Joyce and Gogarty seemed to be engaged in some enterprise. An apostolate of irreverence! The rationalism of Catholicism and the non-rationalism of Protestantism; the nonsensicalness of Irish nationalism, the stupidity of British imperialism were satirized by them in verse and anecdote. What was creative was far from being let off. Joyce's ridicule of my play was to be expected, perhaps, but even Yeats was brought into mocking limericks. That the pair were collaborating on an anthology of inscriptions in public lavatories was known in their set and was regarded as a philosophers' divertissement.

Another time Joyce was among those in the National Library when I was; readers were departing. Timing my exit to be with Joyce's, who was at the turnstile with a friend, ready to leave, I left some volumes on the counter. They were *The World as Will and Idea.* When the three of us were on the stairway, Joyce said with the raillery he often used when addressing me in those days, 'You see before you – two frightful examples of the will to live.' Which meant that Joyce and his companion were out to pick up girls. The companion was taciturn, but I guessed it was he who knew the approaches. We went up Kildare Street and along Harcourt Street to the road off which I lived, the South Circular Road, which, with the lonesomeness of the canal banks adjacent, was a likely place for pickups. As we went along, Joyce talked in a way that was supposed to be a revelation to me of the uncloistered life. In those days he would have relished playing Mephistopheles to Faust; later he was extremely fastidious in his conversation.

His mind mustn't have been totally preoccupied with prospects on the South Circular Road, for after we had cups of tea in a confectioner's in Harcourt Street and went strolling again, we shifted to the World as Idea. Ibsen, remember, was the avatar of the time. I spoke of having seen a non-professional performance of *A Doll's House* and of George Moore's saying to me at the end of it, 'Sophocles! Shakespeare! What are they to this!' Joyce's comment made the elder writer's seem filled with boyish enthusiasm. 'A postcard written by Ibsen will be, regarded as interesting and so will *A Doll's House*. But when we talked of *Hedda Gabler* Joyce showed his admiration for the Master while allowing me to say all the enthusiastic things.

Then he repeated in the original Norwegian a lyric of Ibsen about water lilies. His pronunciation of the words of the poem could not have been, I now realise, any better than that of a German with a few English lessons speaking a lyric of Shakespeare in the original. But as Joyce repeated the lines I had an image of floating flowers brought over into a verse music that I longed to match. The poem that I could never really know became for me a rhythmic challenge.

By this time we had reached the avenue that I lived on; I left the pair, who, as far as I could see, were still without prospects.

No matter how hungry or how shabbily he was dressed, he always had fine composure. His face with the blue eyes was resolved. He would repeat a lyric or a limerick, relate a bawdy incident, or discuss a point in aesthetics in an unruffled, deliberate way. Not even a compliment to his writing could disturb him. Once, when I mentioned that I had read an article of his, he replied in a way that was characteristic of the matter and the manner of his speech: 'I received for it thirty shillings which I immediately consecrated to Venus Pandemos.'

One day Joyce came to me with a request for a loan of a half-sovereign. A financial scheme was involved in its use. He had been given a pawn ticket as a contribution to a fund he was raising for himself. Now, to anyone else a pawn ticket would be a minus quantity, but to Joyce it was realizable. The ticket was for books, and six shillings was the amount they were in for. As the ticket had been contributed by a medical student, Joyce told me, the books were undoubtedly medical, and so of value. And we would take them to our friend George Webb on the Quay, and sell them, and make fifty or even a hundred per cent on the transaction.

So we handed out the money, with its interest, at Terence Kelly's pawnshop, and the books came across the counter to us. Hastily we undid the wrappings. And lo and behold! the books were an unsaleable edition of the Waverley Novels of Sir Walter Scott, with one volume missing.

Sitting outside his shop, with his one closed and his one open eye, George Webb received Joyce cordially. 'Some of your Italian books, Mr. Joyce?' Joyce had taken Italian at University College, spoke it elegantly and fluently, and had picked up a lot of valuable Italian books which he was selling at the time. 'No, Webb; these are special,' replied Joyce. We opened the parcel and exhibited the wretched set of romances. Very loftily indeed did Joyce talk to the most knowing bookseller in Dublin. 'But you have brought some Italian books with you, haven't you, Mr. Joyce?'

When he gathered that Joyce really wanted to sell him the books in the parcel, and that he had ransomed them from Terence Kelly's on the prospect of selling them, Webb had them wrapped up again for us. This most estimable of bookbuyers and booksellers, this George Webb of the swivel eye, was generally found seated meditatively outside his shelves and stacks; he mentioned quietly and firmly the price he would give or take. Across from him on the Quay was the shop of the black-bearded Hickey, who looked like a buccaneer rather than a bookseller, and who would come roaring out of the reaches of his shop, and beat you down if you wanted to sell, or would shamelessly boost the prices marked on the books on the stands outside if you wanted to buy. But George Webb was sympathetic to the book-wanter and the book-disposer. His fairness was recognized. If by chance and unknowingly you brought him the most sought-for book or pamphlet, say Shelley's *Address to the Irish People*, the price he offered you would be the proper price. Now he said mildly to us. 'Take the books back to Terence Kelly's; maybe you can get him to let you have back the six shillings.' We took them back and did manage to get our six shillings.

'I'm not like Jesus Christ – I can't walk on the water,' Joyce said to me the last time I saw him in the National Library. I won't go so far as to say that there was something desperate about him on this occasion, but he was putting on the air of a desperado. Raising funds for his journey to Zurich forced him into a sort of *mendicancy*. He spoke to me of approaching Lady Gregory. I expect he did, but if she helped him, she did it very privately; there is no mention of a gratuity to Joyce in her published correspondence.

Five years after he left Dublin I met the returned James Joyce in O'Connell Street. With him was a little boy, his four-year-old son, Giorgio. In appearance, bearing, manner, Joyce was improved. If I say he was more assured I may be misunderstood, for in one sense Joyce was always assured. But there is a difference between the assurance of a man who has only intellectual capital and the assurance of a man who, besides that, has some sort of position. The Joyce I encountered in the street in 1909 had the assurance of position. He was no longer the 'character', the 'card', the 'artist' of Dublin conversation.

On this first of his visits back to Dublin, I found him as I had known him, or, if altered, a recognizable Joyce. One incident of this particular visit Joyce recalled affectionately, relating it to me years afterward. I remember it as illustrating the strong bond that was between him and his father, a bond of which one strand was music. The incident took place on an excursion made one afternoon by James Augustine Joyce and John Stanislaus Joyce – Stephen Dedalus and Simon Dedalus.

And so, after being five years apart, John Stanislaus Joyce and his son went into the country one afternoon, first taking a tram to the outlying village of Rathfarnham and then walking on. As they went along the quiet country road, the gossip of bars and committee rooms must have been poured into the ear of the author of *Dubliners* and the future begetter of *Ulysses*. A spacious saloon called The Yellow House, some way out into the country, was their terminus. In a big room, empty at the time, there were two pianos. Refreshment having been ordered, the older man sat at one. He played a theme that asked, 'Why did you go from us?' His son, 'Jim', at the other piano, played something in reply (he told me what it was, but I cannot remember). It was an epiphany of a sort, a showing forth of a relationship which was nearly always covered over, and Joyce dwelt on it later with some tenderness. There must have been something in his father that is not revealed in the speech of the Dublin 'character' so bent on 'jollifications'. John Stanislaus Joyce did not impose himself, as Irish fathers thought it was their bounden duty to do, on his son. There was a relationship, and it was not shown overtly, but, as on this occasion, in a very sensitive fashion.

Perhaps it was the day after his excursion with his father that I met James Joyce by appointment in Bewley's Coffee Shop in Westmoreland Street. Bewley's was the afternoon resort of the intelligentsia at that period; it was delightful for its mocha coffee, its freshly baked cakes with fresh butter. Joyce was there ahead of me; I came in with several books under my arm.

At a meeting of this kind Joyce was wont to remain aloof, leaving it to the other person to open up. The books I was carrying were collections of the work of Samuel Ferguson. His centenary was on, and I was writing about him for *Freeman's Journal*. I made an enthusiastic comment about one or two of the poems. Joyce picked up a volume, looking at the poem I mentioned, laid the book down, and like one resigned to his own disability said, 'I couldn't read this.' The suggestion was that he would have liked to.

Joyce reappeared in Dublin later in 1909, to give the city its first moving-picture theatre. I had heard that there was an invention called the cinematograph, which produced continuously moving pictures, but its public functioning was unknown to me. Joyce was the first to explain it all to me, when, hearing he was again in Dublin, I arranged to meet him some-where.

I was impressed when I stood with him inside the building that was being remodelled, and heard him give orders in Italian to the men at work. But I was troubled about one thing. Was this the site for a novel enterprise? Mary Street was on the verge of a slum area. Would people from the residential districts of Dublin come here? I had doubts. I supposed this was the only site available.

His friends did not see much of Joyce that second visit; he was out of Dublin, looking for theatre sites in Belfast and Cork, and when in the city he was busy supervising work in Mary Street, reporting back to Trieste, getting out publicity for this totally new enterprise. As regards the matter that was closest to his heart, the publication of *Dubliners* that did not advance. The proofs, that were to have been given him shortly after his arrival were being held back. In the meantime, the Volta Theatre opened, Dublin saw its first cinema, and Joyce with something outside his own private mission accomplished, went back to Trieste.

Suppose it had been otherwise? Suppose that; when he came back to Dublin this time Joyce had walked into the publishers' office and had been handed the proofs of his first book? Suppose he had gone back to Trieste, with a small cheque on a Dublin bank and a dozen copies of *Dubliners* in his trunk? What a different impression he would have had of his native city? Joyce would have been happier, of course; his mind would have been free of the suspicion of persecution he was prone to. But would there then have been a literature of exile?

The matter of *Dubliners* was still unsettled in the summer of 1912, when Joyce made another visit to Dublin. He spent an evening with my wife and me. Then we received a telegram saying that they were leaving Dublin for Galway that afternoon.

The Joyce whom I spoke to that last afternoon, when the only assistance I could offer him was the name of a man in London, was a Joyce now going into exile in earnest. True, he was going back to a city he had been at home in for a significant part of his life, where he had a wife and two children, not to speak of a brother and sister who had joined him there; he was going back to a place where there were people who were congenial to him. Why, then, did this particular departure come to be marked by him as an unmitigated exile? There is testimony that it was. Years afterward, with his friend the Triestine novelist, Italo Svevo, he was present at a performance of his play in London. "Exiled'? I asked him,' says Svevo. "Exiled. People who return to their home country.' 'But don't you remember,' said Joyce to me, 'how the prodigal son was received by his brother in his father's house. It is dangerous to leave one's country, but still more dangerous to go back to it, for then your fellow-countrymen, if they can, will drive a knife into your heart."

In 1923 my wife and I visited Paris. We called on Joyce at his home. I was curious, on that first visit, to see what changes his long stay away from Ireland had made in him. I noticed a Greek flag on the wall of the vestibule of his apartment. 'The Greeks have always brought me good luck,' he said when I looked enquiringly at it. The flag, he told me, was a relic of Trieste. In that Mediterranean seaport he had spoken to Greeks and learned the Greek vernacular. In Dublin, the then-untravelled Joyce had spoken to me of the Greek epics as being outside European culture; he used to say that the *Divine Comedy* was Europe's epic. It must have been by the Mediterranean that he realised that the first artificer was a Mediterranean man, and it was then that Stephen Hero became Stephen Dedalus.

Our third visit to Paris, after the end of World War I, was in 1927, the fifth year of *Ulysses*. We saw more of Joyce this time than on the previous visit. Reminiscing with the composer of *Work in Progress,* I spoke of being in a Dublin music hall, the Lyric (or was it the Tivoli?), when a gang of students ragged a female performer by tossing at her feet a large corset. She made an indignant rejoinder, declaring that she was a Dublin girl and entitled to decent treatment from Dublin fellows. Maybe it was *because* she was a Dublin girl – residence might have set up a score against her – that there was the immodest demonstration. I didn't think that anyone except myself remembered it, and I remembered it because it was the first and last time I was among what was for me the far from respectable audience of that particular music hall. But Joyce hadn't missed it. With the triumph of a historian who has made a footnote to one of Gibbon's footnotes, he exclaimed: 'I have her in. She is the one who is mad jealous.' The performer's name was Madge Ellis. So there is it. And if I didn't make it public, would the best equipped commentator ever be able to reveal what is behind that 'madjealous' in *Finnegans Wake*?

Once Nora had decreed that 'Jim' was to get himself a new suit, and the three of us took a taxi to a shop near the Galeries Lafayette. Even while trying on pants and jackets under the scrutiny of his wife, Joyce was not completely detached from *Work in Progress*. He laughed like a schoolboy who has inserted a meaningful cipher on the margin of his lessons when I told him I had identified the 'Tantrist' of one of the instalments in *Transition*: he is Tristan the trickster, the one who leaps backward from Iseult's bed. 'I don't know how I can think of such things,' he said, as though delighted with himself.

One evening at dinner I listened to Joyce quote Goldsmith. That the author of *The Vicar of Wakefield* and *The Deserted Village* meant so much to the author of *Chamber Music* and *Ulysses* was something of a discovery.

I was later to make an even more interesting discovery. In the Arts Club, Dublin, a member Mr. George O'Donnell, spoke to me about a book he had since his schooldays at Belvedere College, where he was a classmate of Joyce, on the front page of which Joyce had written a piece about him. He very kindly offered to lend me the book, and I have it before me now. It is *A Concise History of Ireland* by P. W. Joyce, published in 1894. The class in Belvedere had been reading Goldsmith's *Retaliation* and the sixteen-year old Joyce singled out one of his classmates for an address that echoes Goldsmith's mock epitaphs. I believe it is the earliest piece of Joyce's verse that has been found:

G. O'Donnell

Poor little Georgie, the son of a lackey,
Famous for 'murphies' spirits, and 'baccy.

Renowned all around for a feathery head
which had a tendency to become red.
His genius was such that all men used to stare
His appearance was that of a bull at a fair
The pride of Kilmainham, the joy of the class
A moony, a loony, an idiot, an ass.
Drumcondra's production, and by the same rule,
The prince of all pot-boys, a regular fool.
All hail to the beauteous, the lovely, all hail
And hail to his residence in Portland gaol.

Joyce would become genial when he spoke of Goldsmith; he used quote with enjoyment from *Retaliation* the lines about Burke:

'Though fraught with all learning, yet straining
his throat,
To persuade Tommy Townshend to lend him
a vote.'

He was unassuming, Joyce went on to say, praising Goldsmith for personal qualities. He spoke of it as virtue in a man to make no disturbance about what he does or the life he has to live.

At that same dinner, a writer from whom Joyce was supposed to have inherited something – Jonathan Swift – was mentioned. As a Dublin man, if nothing more, Joyce might be expected to offer tribute to Swift. But all he said of him was, 'He made a mess of two women's lives.' When I remarked on Swift's intensity, Joyce said with quiet conviction, 'There is more intensity in a single passage of Mangan's than in all Swift's writing.' (We were all Irish at the table, and so the literary figures discussed were mainly Irish.) Though I could not agree with his estimate of Mangan – for Joyce it was highly extravagant – I was delighted that even now that he was a writer with a European reputation, he had kept his youthful admiration for a poet who is hardly known outside Ireland.

The talk went back to Irish writers. For Yeats' poetry Joyce had – but this was no news – a high regard; he mentioned that he had collaborated on a translation into Italian of *The Countess Cathleen*. Of course I remembered that a lyric from his play, *Who will go drive with Fergus now?* had possessed the mind of Stephen Dedalus at a sorrowful time of his life.

Having spoken of Yeats, Joyce went on to speak of Synge and George Moore. He had also helped to translate Synge's *Riders to the Sea* into Italian. He said he thought the play too short to have a tragic scope. I disagreed with him in this, saying that in the stage production the keening of the women who come into the house gives it another dimension.

George Moore had given Joyce one of his recent books; he was sorry it was not *Esther Waters* which was the novel of Moore he admired. Other names came up as the company talked, Arthur Symons among them. Symons' translations of Verlaine, Joyce took it on himself to say, were equal to the originals.

Joyce and James Stephens were a great deal together about this time. We found this companionship a happy feature of the Joyce establishment during our sojourns in Paris. The author of *Ulysses* had come under the spell of the author of *The Crock of Gold.* And who wouldn't? No one in the world had so much spontaneity with so much gusto as James Stephens, so much wisdom with so much nonsense, so much fantasy with so much poetry.

If he had not been a poet and storyteller, James Stephens would have been a clown in the great style. I would see Joyce looking at him, as Stephens, with his brown eyes and his mobile face, was singing something about 'Mick Mulligan's terrier dog', and would guess a relationship between them that was different from the occult one that Joyce had announced, based on dates and names they had in common. They had an occupational relationship, I thought then, they were both of the company of a group of strolling players. I could see them in a booth or on a stage in the open air, one appearing and singing some great aria, then the other coming on with a monologue composed of poetry and fantasy. What a performance that pair could give!

Joyce's attachment to Stephens was shown by a retort that came from him when I questioned something that Stephens had done. He and Cynthia had left Paris to be house guests of Lady Londonderry. 'Isn't it a wonder,' I said to Joyce, 'that James Stephens would have anything to do with a descendant of Castlereagh?' Joyce did not answer for a moment: then he said with some rancour, 'Haven't I seen you talking with John Dillon's son?'

I will have to explain why the retort was a staggering surprise to me. Lord Londonderry was a descendant of the Castlereagh who, in the most cynical fashion, destroyed the Irish Legislature. John Dillon belonged to the group in Parnell's party that deposed him as leader. In Joyce's time and mine, John Dillon, backed by an Irish constituency, worked for the restoration of the Legislature. That Joyce should put John Dillon and Castlereagh in the same class was inexplicable to me. John Dillon's son was in Paris; he was a philologist studying Sanskrit and the connections of Old Irish with it. My wife and I had brought this young man, Myles Dillon, to Joyce's, and Joyce had treated him with his usual courtesy. And all the time he was remembering that he was entertaining the son of a man who had helped to bring about the downfall of the Uncrowned King!

Pondering on this, I found something magnificent in the unreason of Joyce's loyalty to an individual who had stirred his imagination. What passion a boy of ten or eleven must have known as he watched Parnell's downfall! Was it this that separated him from all political interests? 'Colum, this is the second time I have come into the room and found you talking politics,' he once admonished me.

About this time I wrote an essay on Joyce for *The Dublin Magazine*. Here is how I saw him. He was approaching 50.

'Slender, well-made, he holds himself very upright; he is tastefully dressed, and wears a ring in which there is a large stone. The pupils of his eyes are enlarged because of successive operations, but his gaze is attentive and steady. There is a small tuft of beard on his chin. The flesh of his face has softness and colour – the glow that a child's face has. A detail: his hands have now the softness, the sensitivity, of a man who has to depend a good deal on touch. All the lines of his face are fine; indeed his appearance is not only distinguished but winning. This appearance and his courtesy give him great dignity. Then when one takes note of his appearance one perceives that neither his head nor his forehead is large; the forehead with three deep lines graven on it is narrow, the well-shaped head is small. But head and forehead curve upward and outward, giving a sense of fullness and resonance, each suggesting instrumental amplitude. The jaws close to the chin make the face triangular; they too suggest something in which there is sound. The abundant hair, brushed backward, has lines in it that are like strings, like iron-gray strings.'

One evening at dinner the talk turned on saints, but Joyce would have none of them except St. Patrick. He dismissed Saint Francis. He declared he took little interest in Augustine. Aquinas, then, whose aesthetic the young hero of *Portrait of the Artist* promoted? Joyce would have none of the great Doctor either, or of Saint Ignatius, despite his Jesuit training. The only saint he would praise was Saint Patrick; him he vaunted above all the other Saints in the Calendar. 'He was modest, and he was sincere,' he said, and this was praise indeed from Joyce. And then he added: 'He waited too long to write his *Portrait of the Artist*' – Joyce meant Saint Patrick's *Confession.*

After dinner Joyce sang a tragic and colourful country song I have never come across in any collection, nor heard anyone else sing. It is about a man who has given his wife to a stranger – he may be from Fairyland, he may be Death himself. Joyce learned this song from James Stephens.

'I was going the road one fine day,
Oh, the brown and the yellow ale!
And I met with a man who was no right man;
O love of my heart!
And he said to me, 'Will you lend me your love
For a year and a day, for a year and a day?'
Oh, the brown and the yellow ale,
The brown and the yellow ale.

Those refrains in Joyce's voice had more loss in them than I have ever heard in any other singer's. He once said to me, 'A voice is like a woman – you respond or you do not; its appeal is direct.' He said this to show that what was sung transcended in appeal everything that was written. His own voice in the humorous and the sorrowful songs was unforgettable.

In December of 1931 Joyce's father, John Stanislaus Joyce, died in Dublin. He had done little, as a father, for his eldest son – in fact he had done nothing – but Joyce cherished his image and the memory he had of the musical, sporting, irresponsible, entertaining man. A few years after the publication of *Ulysses* Joyce had commissioned a Dublin artist, Patrick Tuohy, to paint a portrait of his father. The old man lived on a realized insurance with perhaps an old-age pension. Like many old men in Dublin who had some sort of position, he lived not in a lodging house, or a boarding house, but with a family, which, in those days, could let him have board and room for twenty-five or thirty shillings a week.

Not long after John Stanislaus' funeral, I happened to be going from Paris to Dublin, and Joyce asked me to call on the family with whom his father had roomed. It was his hope, I think, that I would bring back some remembrance of the man on whom Simon Dedalus in *Portrait of the Artist* was based. I wrote to the head of this family when I got to

Dublin, telling him I'd like to see him and talk about his late tenant. I had intended to visit him, so that I could get some impression of John Stanislaus' last surroundings, but instead he came to see me.

He was a nice young man who gave the impression that in his domicile the old man had been taken care of, but as he talked about him, the emphasis was on the effort he and his wife had made to keep him decently. To him John Stanislaus Joyce was a battered, shabby old person who had come to live with them after some kind of a breakdown – either an accident such as befalls old men or a shock that had left him somewhat astray. The young man knew that his tenant had meant something to the outside world, for a portrait painter had been in to put him on canvas, and a newspaperman to interview him, but the John Stanislaus whom his son wanted to hear about had never existed for this young Dubliner.

So my report, when I got back to Paris, was disappointing, and I think I, as its bearer, was disappointing, too, to Joyce. Here was I in an apartment that had on the wall Tuohy's *Portrait of a Dublin Gentleman* and other portraits of men and women of his family. And I was making my report to one for whom the tradition of gentlemanliness was important.

Joyce and I went for walks together, Joyce sometimes silent, sometimes conversing. I realized how tragically lonely great fame can leave a man. But I

also remember oddities of discourse on these prom-
enades. Why did Joyce have to be abusive about
nuns? Why did he think that nuns ranked with
tailors in a sort of nullity? He reminded me: 'They
have no office in the Church. They can't even assist
at Mass like altar boys.' He did not mention that one
of his sisters was a nun. She was in a convent in New
Zealand, and from what I heard from one who had
visited her, she had an affection for James; for she
kept as a relic the surplice he wore as a boy when he
served at Mass. (The mention of Joyce as an acolyte
reminds me that no exegete has noticed in his prose
the cadences of the Latin responses to the celebrant,
broken by the ringing of a bell in an unfilled chapel.)
A priest among passers-by drew a favourable comment from Joyce on the garb of French priests. They
wore soft hats. 'If somebody would kidnap the silk
hats of the priests in Ireland, wouldn't that be a gain
for the Church?' he remarked.

Then came Munich, and a shamefaced relief was
evident, at least at first, among the sojourners in
Paris. The Joyces came back to the city. When Joyce
telephoned me, he mentioned the settlement. 'Give
him Europe?' he said angrily. At this time Joyce was
instrumental in trying to place some relatives of a
Jewish friend of his, Herr Brauchbar, whom he had
known in Trieste. Brauchbar had been helpful to
Joyce. Joyce did not forget it. As a result of Joyce's
pleading, I wrote to the Minister of Justice in Ire-

land. After initial setbacks, Herr Brauchbar's relative was permitted to take up residence in Ireland.

In Paris, my wife and I had our last dinner with the Joyces. As the evening drew to a close, Joyce was able to distract his wife's attention while he got the waiter to bring him another bottle of white wine. I conducted him downstairs and had him back and at the table in time to finish his wine before Nora, who had also retired, reappeared. She found him standing before the bowing waiters, whom as usual he had tipped extravagantly.

We were obliged soon afterward to leave Paris for New York. We had boarded the boat train when, looking out of the window we saw Joyce and Nora coming along the platform.

'Good-bye, Joyce! Luck to *Finnegans Wake*,' we called. As the train began to move, Joyce, stumbling on a bit, said to my wife, 'We don't want you to go, but anyhow, you'll be safe in America.'

Padraic Colum

Arthur Power

Like his hero Ulysses, Joyce was a man of many habitations. When I met him first he was living in a gloomy iron-shuttered flat in the Boulevard Raspail. In the centre of the sittingroom was a huge red lampshade spread out like a flounced petticoat, while in the corner my attention was attracted to a collection of sickly yellow plants standing in a corner, wondering if the last tenant had left them as a legacy to the unfortunates who were to follow him. However, one discovered that Joyce attached great importance to them. 'They are phoenix palms,' he told me, 'and remind me of the Phoenix Park, but I cannot keep them alive in this damned brothel,' he added mournfully while I gazed in mute amazement at the author's all embracing imagination. This was the first occasion I had visited Joyce at home; but it was not my first meeting with him. That had taken place at the Bal Bullier, a famous dance hall opposite the café of the 'Closerie de Lilas'.

On the evening in question I had gone there to meet a party which, however, did not materialize; and I wandered about the hall watching the couples dancing, thinking perhaps I might meet someone I knew to dance with. I saw a group of people at the far end of the hall, I knew, but I did not want to get in with them, I wanted to dance; life is too short to talk it away. However, towards the end, one of the ladies hailed me over, and introducing her friends who sat at the table, presented me to James Joyce.

I liked the man; slight and gracefully built, with a rather shakespearian head, he wore strong glasses, which greatly magnified one eye. A small goatee beard covered a thin lipped, curiously shaped mouth. His hands were noticeably fine, and slight fingered. Everything of him proclaimed a poet, – everything except his mouth. His manner was sympathetic rather than friendly – because Joyce's social manner was not easy. He surrounded himself normally with a kind of mental barbed wire – but his exquisite manners, reminiscent of the Dublin of the Grand Days. That remarkable Irish courtliness, he always had. And the more difficult the position was the more perfect was his manner. It had the detachment and nobility to it of a grandee, and was as superior as a diamond is to glass to what passes for manners among provincial gentry and nobility. It was the outward sign of inward refinement; and like all remarkable men he had no conceit; no boorish arrogance.

He asked me if I was 'a man of letters?' The question 'man of letters', had a curiously old-fashioned nineteenth century tang to it, in the rough and tumble of a popular dance hall it sounded like an invitation to a minuet if only an intellectual one. I told him I was interested but did little myself.

'What are you trying to write?' he asked.

I told him that I was interested in the eighteenth century French satirists, and I wanted to write like them.

'You'll never do it,' he said, 'never – you are an Irishman – you must write in an Irish tradition; write what is in your blood, and not what is in your head.'

I told him I was tired of nationality. I wanted to become international – all great writers were international.

'Yes – but they were national first – if you are sufficiently national you will be international.'

We rose to go out, and I gathered that the party was to celebrate the fact that an American publisher, a Miss Beach, had agreed to publish his new book, *Ulysses*. He had spent seven years writing it, in Rome, in Zürich, in Paris; and having it written, he had had no idea who would undertake its publication. Now Miss Beach had agreed to do it. We stopped for a while at the 'Café des Lilas', on the high terrace facing the miniature wood which fills that corner of the boulevard and drank 'tilleuls' before returning home. Joyce spoke of the power of language; and he compared the English language to an organ for its sonorous wealth. Several of us protested that we preferred the French language for its precision and musical quality. But he would not agree, and to support his argument he quoted passages of the English Bible, and then quoted corresponding passages out of the French text.

Joyce had a marvellous memory, and he could

quote stanzas of poetry on end. To support his argument now he quoted passages from the Authorized Version.

'And He came and touched the bier, and they that bore him stood still. And He said: 'Young man, I say to thee, arise'.'

– Et s'étant approché, il toucha la bière, et ceux qui la portaient s'arrêtèrent, et il dit: 'Jeune homme, je te dis, lève-toi.' And Joyce compared the weakness of 'Je te dis, lève-toi' with – 'I say unto thee, arise'... and he went on to compare two longer passages, for Joyce was nothing if he was not thorough, out of Matthew, quoting the English version first –

'Whereof if thy right hand or thy foot offend thee, cut them off, and cast them from thee; it is better for them to enter life halt or maimed rather than having two hands or two feet to be cast into everlasting fire.'

And then the French version.

'Que si ta main ou ton pied te fait tomber dans le pêche, coupe les: et jette les loin de toi; car il vaut mieux que tu entres boiteux ou manchot dans la vie, que d'avoir deux pieds ou deux mains, et d'être jeté le feu éternel.'

He remarked how superior in language, in music, and strength, was the English version to the French.

It was an argument in which one required a very good memory so as to be able to quote numerous and similar passages in the two languages, and none of us were equal to it; so we relinquished it, leaving the palms of victory with him, but secretly holding to our own opinion as in all arguments between opposing ideas.

After that I did not see him for some time. The next flat I visited him in was in the Avenue Charles Floquet. This, in contrast, was a fine airy apartment, and the most attractive of his many habitations. It looked out on to the Eiffel Tower opposite, and since it was near the Ecole Militaire through the trees one occasionally caught glimpses of uniformed officers riding past in the Parc du Champs de Mars.

But unfortunately Joyce's eyes were very bad at that time, and as likely as not when one entered one would find him lying on a bed, the blinds drawn, stooping his eyes in the darkened room, when he would wisecrack 'that he was waiting for Irelands Eye to do its duty'.

Then towards evening he would get up, when I would accompany him down town in a taxi to his occulist Dr. Borach who had his consulting-rooms in the Rue de la Paix. Going up a private back stairs we would wait in a small badly papered room evidently reserved for V.I.P.'s. Presently, after a time Dr. Borach, a soft-looking silent-moving man, who looked as though he had never taken a draught of fresh air in his life, would enter in a hurry, examine Joyce's eyes with a lens, make a few remarks, and tell him to call again in two days time. Then we would descend those narrow backstairs again, and hailing a taxi, drive to the Café Francis. This Café looked across the Seine and faced the ornate Pont de l'Alma supported by those famous sculpted Zouaves which also act as hydrometres in the temperamental Seine and warn Parisians of possible inundations.

This café was a favourite haunt of Joyce's at this time, and here he would drink a Cinzano-à-l'eau, its rich ruby colour being more evocative than its alcoholic content, and discuss Irish literature, Dublin, and the disadvantages of possessing a Celtic temperament. After a while we would return to the flat where Mrs. Joyce would provide an excellent dinner, chicken cooked in wine being a 'spécialité de la maison'.

Indeed some of my happiest memories are of sitting down to this family meal with his son, the foreign-mannered and dapper Giorgio just coming to be a young man, and the young Lucia, silent and sensitive, but gay nevertheless, and with no shadow of the subsequent tragedy which was to fall so unexpectedly on her.

And if report has it that in Dublin, Trieste, and Pola, Joyce had been wild and uncontrollable in his youth, when his friend Alessandro Francini would find him lying almost senseless in the gutters of the città vecchia of Trieste, now he gave the impression of being calm and settled, confident even; that is, as confident as he ever was, for strangely enough his confidence was inclined to ebb and flow with the tides of his temperament. For though he had braved and flaunted all accepted social and literary conventions in that great scoffing book of his, yet at times, it seemed, that like all sensitive men he would secretly query the ultimate value of his talent, his spirit weakening for the moment under the blast of an adverse criticism, perhaps; or from some secret psychological cause. It is something which others have noticed also. To my mind, anyway, it was one of the most attractive and human things about him, when collapsing on a seat with those much magnified eyes fixed questioningly on you he would repeat some malicious criticism he had read. The one which seems to have affected him most was the statement that he was a middle-class writer, whatever that may mean, but which in the pre-war world of fascism sounded like the threatening beat of a drum.

But on meeting him a few days later one would know by the gleam in his eye and the way he turned his head that his confidence – his superconfidence, in fact – in his talent had returned.

Also, I think that he felt sure that in Paris – the last of the human cities as he described it, – when his work came to be published it would be more appreciated than anywhere else. Intellectually Paris is a city without prejudice, whatever its current political ferment might be. At that time the atmosphere owing to the continual hargle-bargle going on over

Reparations was, as often as not, violently anti-British. So intense was it at times that it met you like a wave when you went out into the street; for French emotionalism can run swift and high.

But already during his short stay he had made a number of friends and staunch adherents such as Pound, Miss Beach, and the French writers Gide, and Valery Larbaud.

Indeed Larbaud was so enthusiastic that on reading some extracts from the courageous American *Little Review,* as well as the typescript of *The Oxen of the Sun* which Miss Beach had sent him, he wrote to her, 'I am raving mad over *Ulysses.* It is as great comprehensive, and human as Rabelais,' adding that since he had read it he had been unable to write, or sleep; he proposed to translate some pages to go with an article on the author in the Nouvelle Revue Française, at that time the most influential literary magazine in France.

One of the many things which intrigued French writers, and in fact the writers and intellectuals of all nations alike, was that Joyce's book was based on Homer's Odyssey, his hero's adventures, if you can call Bloom a hero, paralleling those of the wily Greek king. I remember once, for instance, how he compared the barmaids in the Ormond Hotel and the Sirens, saying that the barmaids were fine only to the waist with a careful hair-do, and make-up, and fresh well-laundered blouses, but below the waist they were fish-tailed, wore dirty old skirts, rough mended stockings, and broken comfortable shoes, all which were not seen, of course.

So the analogy is worked out from chapter to chapter, starting with the Telemachus Episode in the Martello Tower at Sandycove; to the Nestor in Mr. Deasy's school; the Proteus, 'the old man of the sea' in the Sandymount Strand episode; The Sirens in the Ormond bar and 'sonnez-la-cloche'; and on to the final episode of Penelope in which according to Vico's philosophy a semi-goddess is shrunk to normal size.

Indeed on meeting Joyce himself one could not but be reminded that his wandering existence was similar to that of his chosen hero travelling as he had done from country to country and from town to town; and now in Paris from flat to flat, and from hotel to hotel, to say nothing of his numerous departures down into the French countryside to Nice, Burgundy, Brittany, and even into Holland and Switzerland; always restless, and always seeking. Indeed I remember him telling me on his return how while he had been staying down at Chartres he had listened with relish one evening to the conversation of some local women as they had washed the clothes against the stones in the river, a conversation which he later incorporated into the famous monologue of 'Anna Livia Plurabelle'.

'Tuck up your sleeves and loosen your talk-tapes.

And don't butt me – hike when you bend. Or whatever it was they threed to make out he thried to two in the Fiendish Park. He's an awful old reppe. Look at the shirt of him! Look at dirt of it.'

As we know, he finally placed the scene, as he placed everything, back in Dublin – this Dublin which he never left in his imagination, and which he had hated and even despised in his tormented youth, but which after long exile he had re-found to cherish; now a sort of half-real and half dream city; for Dublin was to Joyce what Florence was to Dante, the city of his soul.

Another novelty about *Ulysses* which intrigued contemporary writers was what he called his 'telegraphic style'; short pungent sentences which he considered the proper ones for the present day; a sort of literary infra-red ray in which he figured everything as in a cubist picture, even to the very larva of life.

'Ulysses is not a hero' – a priest had said to him at Clongowes. But Joyce thought he was, on his own terms, for he had always admired this wily wanderer who had surmounted his difficulties with determination and cunning; as stoically as Ulysses Joyce had condemned himself for years to such thankless tasks as keeping books, teaching, and working in a Bank rather than sell his talent, suffering from the continual snubs and frustrations of publishers but never losing sight of his ultimate purpose, constantly carrying this image of Dublin with him wherever he went, determined once and for all to break down the classical and romantic image which had dominated literature for so long.

It was the Medieval and the Medievalists which attracted him most. I remember one day walking with him down the Boulevard St. Michel. On our left rose the spire of the Sainte Chapelle with that angel poised on its summit which always seems just to have alighted; while further down was the ancient Monastery of the Cluny, and those huge and sinister hulks of masonry the remains of the original wall of Paris. 'It was the true spirit of Europe,' he said, 'think of the magnificent civilization we would have had if we had remained in that tradition' – He looked on the Renaissance and its return to classicism as a return to intellectual boyhood. 'Compare,' he continued, 'a medieval building with a classical one, Notre Dame with La Madelaine, for instance; Notre Dame with plane countering plane, roof against roof, its flying buttresses, and erupting gargoyles.' He maintained that the present age was gradually returning to medievalism, remarking finally, with some bitterness, that if he had lived in the 14th or 15th century he would have been much more appreciated.

Also the Ireland he had known, in his opinion, was still medieval, and Dublin a medieval city in which the sacred and the obscene jostled shoulders.

'Show a Renaissance work to an Irish peasant,' he exclaimed, 'and he gazes at it in cold wonder, for it is not his world'; he would point out how Yeats was a typical medievalist with his interest in magic, his Countess Cathleens, and his belief in signs and symbols, and his later bawdiness... 'And it is this which separates an Irishman from Englishmen, Frenchmen, Italians, and from the rest of Europe, for we have never been subjected to the Lex Romanus, nor are we Renaissance men.'

I remember when talking to him in Paris once I was explaining my uncertainty as on what creative lines to proceed, amid all the confusing and, it seemed, jarring claims, of Modernity. He recommended study of *The Book of Kells*. 'Wherever I have been,' he said, 'in whatever pass of life, or circumstances, I have always carried that with me and gone to it for inspiration. You can compare much of my work to the intricate designs of its illuminations, and I have pored over its workmanship for hours at a time in Dublin, in Trieste, in Rome, in Geneva – wherever I have been, and I have always got inspiration from it.

Also when talking about literature he maintained that a country must be vintaged before it could produce literature – in other words, it must have an odour... 'the first thing you notice when you visit a country is its smell, and in literature Rabelais smells of Medieval France; Chaucer of the England of the

Middle Ages; Don Quixote of Spain; and *Ulysses* smells of the Dublin of my day.'

'It certainly has an effluvia,' I told him.

'Yes, it smells of Anna Liffey – not always a sweet smell but a pungent one all the same.'

'Also,' he remarked, 'you must remember that we are an uninhibited race seldom behaving or thinking as convention demands.' He quoted Bernard Shaw as a typical example. 'Restraint is irksome to us, and that is what gives us our originality; had we been allowed to develop our own Celtic civilization instead of this mock English one imposed on us, and which has never suited us, think of what an original interesting civilization we might have produced. Indeed, it is my revolt against the English conventions, literary and otherwise that is the main source of my talent.'

Also talking of writing, he said that he did not believe in planning it all beforehand on the classsical formula, for, as he said, 'the good thing comes in the writing – words create' or, to use the French imagist poet Mallarmé's phrase – 'leave the initiative to them'.

But, on the other hand, he believed in writing dangerously. 'For Classicism is dead,' he declared. 'It was the art of the gentlemen, and gentlemen are out of date.'

Another very important issue with him, and for which he suffered much, was the liberation of literature. English speaking puritanism had restricted the freedom of the author, the freedom they had had on the Continent for centuries. This he was determined to break down, and because he flouted the Anglo-Saxon conventions he was prosecuted, banished, and finally burnt as a heretic in a kind of intellectual auto-da-fé. But he looked on himself as in the tradition of writers like Chaucer, Brantome, Rabelais, Maupassant, and others. Yet I think it was something that made him shy and diffident in company, for I remember him saying to me, 'You know there are people who would refuse to sit in the same room with me.'

As we know, the printers in England refused to print his book, and the Editors of the *Little Review* in America were prosecuted and fined, even though two of the judges had to admit publicly that the particular passages read to them were incomprehensible. And it was Miss Beach who finally agreed to print and publish *Ulysses* in France with Darantiere, a friend of Mlle. Mounier's. That party at the Ball Bullier, where I had first met Joyce, had been the occasion to celebrate the signing of the contract between them.

After this I did not see him for some time (being away in Ireland most probably), and when we did meet again he was staying in a hotel close to the Gare Montparnasse. When I entered the hotel room where he was, I found him lying on the bed with the blinds drawn, surrounded by a collection of half-written manuscripts undergoing one of his difficult periods, miserable in soul and body. Indeed, one could not help wondering how he could work under these conditions; a lift continually grinding up and down outside his door; the noise and bustle of luggage being wheeled along the passage outside; a child crying in the next room; but persisting as he had always persisted! Yeats' lines from *Nineteen Hundred and Nineteen* came to me:

> 'O man in his own secret meditation,
> Is lost amid the labyrinth that he has made
> In art or politics.'

However, apart from his eye trouble, I need not have commiserated with him, for he told me that he preferred to work surrounded by activity – 'honest to God activity', as he remarked pointedly, and that he had found it impossible to work in the silence and security of that room especially designed for writing, which Larbaud had lent him, near the Luxemburg Gardens; a room I once visited with him to collect some manuscripts. Built in the foundations of a house it was fashioned like the bunk on a ship with a long table down the centre. Cool in summer; owing to its small size it could easily be heated in winter, and it had seemed to me ideal in every way. But its very noiselessness had made it impossible for him to work there.

However, he did not remain much longer in this hotel, for shortly afterwards he had to undergo yet another operation from the ever ready hands of Dr. Borsch, when he entered the clinic in the Rue du Cherche-Midi. Here I visited him, lying in a small low-ceilinged room with one single dim light burning over his bed. Its general dilapidated appearance surprised and dismayed me, belonging as it did to a leading occulist, conditions which prompted Joyce to compose the following verse:

'The clinic was a patched one,
Its outside old as rust
And every place beneath that roof
Lay four feet thick in dust.'

But what worried him most of the time was that he thought that with its constant use he had contracted Atropine poisoning. He asked me to hunt up a book for him on the subject, fearing as he did the effect it might have on his brain. But when I called again with a book on poisons borrowed out of the American library, someone had forestalled me with a small library on the subject.

In the meantime, Mrs. Joyce had been hunting for a suitable flat which at last they found at 2 Square Robiac in a cul-de-sac running off the rue de Grenelle not very far from the former Charles

Floquet; here he remained for seven years, longer than in any other place; here they had their own furniture, and at last he was able to install his family pictures which with Celtic reverence he had carried all round Europe; old-fashioned Georgian portraits by Comerford of Cork, of serious and respectable looking women wearing big bonnets tied under the chin. One which I particularly remember was of a fine looking old gentleman in a red hunting coat and a white stock, a relation of Daniel O'Connell, so Joyce said, – all these have since been lost when his effects were sold up by the landlord during the war to pay the rent – portraits which breathed of country houses, farmlands, horses, tea-parties, visits to fairs and to church; the usual country round of succession and tradition out of which had unexpectedly risen this light-limbed rebel.

It is this flat which one associates with him more than any other, perhaps because he lived in it for so long, and it was the one in which I visited him most constantly.

Also at the time he decided that he wanted to have his father's portrait painted in Dublin to add to the collection, and asked me to recommend an artist. I suggested Paul Henry, Leo Whelan and others, but he did not respond. Then the name of Patrick Tuohy occurred to me. 'Yes,' he said – deciding on the moment – 'I think I know his father, Doctor Tuohy – I will have him do it' – a queer touch of provincialism, so it seemed to me at the time.

However, when it arrived it turned out to be a very good portrait of the old reprobate sitting in his armchair with his tugged moustache and fierce rheumy eyes, all Dublin's gossip bubbling on his broken lips – Ulysses incarnate.

Then Tuohy came over to Paris to paint the entire Joyce family. But his personality irritated Joyce so that when Tuohy talked to him about painting his soul, Joyce answered him shortly, 'Don't worry about my soul, but get my tie straight.' Also he asked him point blank once – 'Do you want to paint me, or my name?'

And every time one went into the flat one was sure to find Tuohy at all hours sitting on the floor checking one of his portraits in a mirror. In fact he seriously upset the rhythm of Joyce's life. Also, he was inclined to irk Joyce in annoying ways, jibing, that he should now write 'a best seller'.

But Tuohy was mentally a sick man, for he confided to me that he had an ulcer on his palate which was eating into his brain. I suggested he should consult a doctor. 'They are no use,' he answered me hopelessly.

After his stay in Paris, Tuohy went to America to the Southern States, and then moved up to New York, where one day, poor fellow, he pasted up his studio with newspapers and turned on the gas. When I told Joyce of his death he replied coldly, 'He nearly made me commit suicide too' — a remark of unusual bitterness for him.

Another picture he had in his flat was Vermeer's picture of Ghent, of the river flowing past the quays lined with those quaint red brick houses which, like *Ulysses,* was a picture of a city, and so had a particular significance for him. But in general he was not much interested in art for like many other writers, I think, he regarded it as inferior, and I remember as we walked down the narrow Rue du Seine with the buses roaring behind our backs, I used to stop before the picture dealers' windows and point out the latest Braque or Modigliani trying to raise his enthusiasm. But after looking at them for a while he would only ask 'How much are they worth?' which I am certain was intended for a sarcasm.

Indeed, not only did he appear not to be interested in modern art, then the rage in Paris, but he also ignored the multiple artistic activity that went on around him. The Russian Ballet for instance... Parade... Caisse Noisettes... and Stravinsky's electric *Sacre du Printemps* in which the movement of the dancers was like that of a rugby scrum when, at the end, a single figure emerges to dance the pas-seul of Spring.

Indeed at one of the opening performances I remember a fight starting in the audience among those who were in favour of it, and those who were against, and as I stood in the bar afterwards I saw a girl pass by, her evening dress half torn off; I must say I could not but secretly admire a race who took their art so seriously.

But Joyce only went once or twice. He said it was a passing fashion, and seemed to despise the furore it had created.

The one art besides literature he really cared about was music; for Dubliners have always been crazy about music. They will queue for hours to see a visiting opera company; and what they liked and still do, are the old-fashioned operas by Verdi, Donizetti, Cimarosa, and Rossini, the Italian 'bel canto'.

It was the tenor voice he admired; I never heard him admire a woman's voice, a Gallicurchi or a Melba; in fact when I knew him he was inclined to be cynical about women in general, for once in a moment of innocent enthusiasm, I asked him what Italian women were like – 'Cold,' he replied, 'like all women.'

It was the male voice which attracted, and this accounted for his admiration of Sullivan, the Irish tenor, which became an obsession in the end; he would worry all his influential friends to go and hear Sullivan, and eventually through his persistent efforts succeeded in getting him on to Covent Garden, but only for one or two performances, I think. I never heard this singer, but Budgeon, his friend and biographer, is reported to have said, 'he had a voice like the Forth Bridge'; and Jo Davidson said much the same thing. But Joyce thought he was the greatest of tenors, maintaining obstinately that no voice like his had been heard for fifty years, seeing in him perhaps, his own frustrated ambition.

Indeed, all the Joyce family sang; his father, himself, and his son whom he had trained as a singer – so that one could truly say with Joyce that where there was no singing there was no joy. One of my lasting memories of him is how somewhere about midnight he used to cross the room in the same Square Robiac, and sitting down at the piano try his hand on the keyboard letting his fingers run in a musical ripple over the notes when he would sing in his light tenor voice those mocking, ironic, and melancholy Irish songs, a fundamental source of his inspiration, and whose threads he wove and re-wove to form the dark and complicated tapestry of *Finnegans Wake*, songs which like his family portrait he carried with him everywhere he went, and finally turned to for consolation.

Lucia, his daughter, took up dancing. I saw her dance several times, and she promised very well. Once at an international concourse at the Bal Bullier, if she did not get first prize, she was acclaimed by the audience who cried out in enthusiasm, 'L'Irlandaise – L'Irlandaise.' But her father was against it. He thought that she lacked the necessary physical qualifications, and said something about 'women getting up on the stage and waving their arms about', and remarked that 'a girl should learn to walk into a room properly, that is enough'. She gave it up, and at his suggestion took up book illumination. But in secret she was frustrated. The trouble with the children of a famous man is that they are inclined to suffer from a continual inferiority complex. Everyone is interested in the father, and not in them; and though Joyce tried to draw her into the current of life, she resisted secretly and was only willing, as was natural, to accept life on her own terms.

But I remember her as a sensitive and silent girl sitting at the restaurant table, reminding me rather of one of Marie Laurencin's demoiselles, mysterious and evasive, though later I believe she became troublesome and dominant; and as her illness increased, she became to his dismay more hostile to him while he tried to retain her affection in circumstances of increasing difficulty. For Joyce, for whom Creation, Origin, and Paternity, were the secret of being, no tragedy could have gone deeper, and the image of his sick child tortured him, for with his peculiar theories of paternity he considered himself as the father, the guilty source. He took her from clinic to clinic, even to Professor Jung in Switzerland, who as a matter of fact, disliked Joyce and his works, and had jibed that *Ulysses* meant as much read backwards as forwards, and that at any other time in the past it would never have reached the printer; Lucia herself expressed her own resentment of Jung by saying – 'to think that such a big fat materialistic Swissman should try and get hold of my soul.'

But Joyce, as her father, thought that he understood her best. He hoped by some miracle of paternal love that he would bring about her cure, for she acted on him as the ghost had acted on Hamlet.

Around Joyce in Paris were collected a number of progressive writers; Americans for the most part. One was Hemingway, a tall, well-built, handsome fellow, in whose swagger was something of a buccaneer. He was then making his first essays in original prose, an expression of the American mind, differing as it does from the European mind. In Joyce's flat at the periodical reading of his 'work in progress' he used to be there bringing with him a fine fresh-air atmosphere, with his big gestures and a resonant laugh.

I remember once he and Padraic Colum, the Irish writer, having a joke about their not having a 'carte d'identité'. Padraic had found a woman's purse, evidently that of a poor woman, in the taxi on his way to Joyce's flat, and was very anxious to return it to the police station.

'But have you got a 'carte d'identité'?' he asked.

No, he had not one.

'Then,' I told him, 'I would not go to the police station if I were you. They won't care a rap about the purse, but they will put you in prison for not having a 'carte d'identité'.'

'That's true,' joined in Hemingway; 'you can do nothing without it. A man can come and hit you in the face, but you dare not hit him back because you have not got a 'carte d'identité' – a man can knock you down, he can take your money, your wife, – but if you have no...' But further elaboration was cut short by Joyce in his white coat, a short white coat like a dentist's which he always wears when working, sitting down at a table, and wearing very strong spectacles, to read the manuscript of some 'work in progress'. After listening awhile to this strange incantation, which I take it represents the sleep or nocturnal consciousness, as Ulysses represents the fantastical day consciousness, of the city, I turned and looked surreptiously at my fellow-listeners, and wondered what they were thinking. Hemingway sat looking straight before him, resolute and determined like a Roman soldier, showing little outward evidence of his modernity; Colum, elusive, but sympathetic, his round head, which always had a boyish air, drooped to one side.

Meanwhile, Joyce had quitted his flat in the Square Robiac, and in the course of his endless peregrinations had gone to London to arrange his remarriage. I visited him there and found him living at this time in a dark and uncomfortable flat in Camden Grove in Kensington, a place which he nicknamed 'Camden Grave'. But after a few months he left it to return to Paris to a place in the Avenue

St. Philibert. But what with his increasing troubles now added by the news of his father's death in Dublin which he took very badly, the stage now began to darken for him so that he composed a new tragic but not unhumorous calendar of the weekdays starting with – 'Moansday, Tearsday, Wailsday, Thumpsday, Frightday, Shatterday'.

Then, the lease of that flat falling in, he took himself, his wife, and Lucia, off to Switzerland; he for his eyes, and Lucia for psychiatric treatment. When again they returned to Paris they fixed themselves in the Rue Galilée, off the Champs Elysées. And it was here that I met him for the last time, calling one afternoon.

I had not seen him for several years for I had been living in Waterford, battling with the difficulties of running the family estate, a constant daily round of farming and also trying to maintain a disintegrating Georgian mansion a thousand miles away from the Parisian world of art and letters, where the names of Modigliani, Pascin, Braque, had never been heard of, and even that of Joyce was but a faint echo.

He invited me that evening to Fouquets, an expensive restaurant, the most expensive, in fact, on the Champs Elysées, which he now frequented. Sitting at the far end of the table surrounded by the fashionable clientele, detached and observant. I watched Joyce sipping his wine surrounded by the Jolas family who had then taken possession of him.

But I felt a gulf had risen between us as was natural perhaps over so many years, and due to such different experiences, while the atmosphere which surrounded him seemed to me to be very artificial. From what I could overhear of the conversation, it seemed to consist chiefly of quibbling over the possible extension in the meaning of individual words, and suchlike literary hair-splitting. Joyce noticed my attitude and remarked not without justice – 'You look more and more like a farmer' – which was fair enough. I had not liked *Finnegans Wake* and had told him so. Indeed worse I thought, though I had remained silent about it, that he had wasted many vital creative years and would perhaps have done better to have taken Tuohy's sarcastic advice; but then, what do we know of the strange psychological changes an artist may undergo.

Next day, I called to say goodbye. Collapsing as was his habit on a seat in the hall he repeated some of the criticisms that had been levelled against his work, quoting Wyndham Lewis's jibe about him being a middle-class writer, something I did not and could not understand, and which had a Fascist origin anyway; but, there for a moment, I was face to face with the former human and ever-kind Joyce, free from that coterie of hangers-on and publicists for ever busy sunning themselves on his fame; the man of Dublin, Trieste, Pola, and those early days in Paris, still unchanged. I thought how fame, like a

always kind and friendly, and who through the troubled sea of married life from the darkness of obscurity to the high-lights of fame had always managed to hold her family together with her courage, and rock-firm common sense. It is true that she was not an intellectual in any sense; and why should she be? But nevertheless, she was a sincere and gallant woman, and his worthy companion and mate – this breath of Galway air in the intellectual hothouse of Paris.

In April 1951 she died of uremic poisoning brought on by the treatment for her arthritis, and she was buried in the same cemetery as her husband, but, typical of their wandering life, some way apart. I believe that has been rectified, and, re-interred, they lie side by side in the snow-covered Fluntern cemetery outside the lake-reflecting town of Zürich where so much of *Ulysses* was conceived and written.

And so that story ends; so ends the life of this extraordinary man who mirrored back the life of his native city with zest, humour, mimicry, and devilment, and who during his life refused all compromise and concession, who hated any form of narrow-mindedness, and who as an artist never faltered or wrote a commercial line. And when the golden carpet would have been laid out for him wherever he cared to go, he shut himself up into a monumental silence, and set himself to write his new work, still wandering as his Greek hero had wandered, yet al-

marionette, turning in a glitter before the public gaze is only a projection of a personality so to speak, while its projector, the real man of flesh and blood continues to live his everyday life in spite of, and even contrary to it, escaping nothing. And as I turned to go down the stairs, we both raised our hands on what was to be a final farewell.

Then, in the papers, one read of his hegira in the terror and confusion of war to Switzerland, and to Zürich where he still hoped to find peace and security, remembering his former days there during the 1914 war, while Hitler's demoniac world crashed slowly but inevitably to pieces around him.

For some years he had been suffering from internal pains which his American friends had diagnosed wrongly as of nervous origin which suited Joyce. It was, however, a duodenal which perforated. An emergency operation was carried out, and he seemed to recover, but, passing into a coma, he died without regaining consciousness.

Some years later I happened to be in Paris when I met Nora, his wife, who had come there on business. I asked her where she would like to go and dine. She said 'The Café Francis'. But it was a mistake, and that evening was a very unhappy one for her with former memories crowding in. As she limped painfully to the waiting taxi, I heard her mutter aloud, 'this too, too solid flesh', for she did not want to continue; this charming, natural woman,

ways fixed in his purpose, carrying with him as a
seafarer might carry some magic talisman to bring
him at last safely to his destination – this image of
his island home.

Arthur Power

'almost in the middle of Ireland'. Father master of a workhouse. Though he grew up in Dun Laoighaire beside Dublin, Padraic Colum spent part of his early life in the Midlands which gave him his feeling for the countryside. Wrote his first play when he was twenty. His second play written when he was still young, *The Land* was the first successful play of the Irish Theatre movement. He followed this with *The Fiddlers House* and *Thomas Muskerry*.

In 1914 he went to the United States. In 1923 on the invitation of the Hawaiian Legislature he went to that country to make a survey of their traditional stories. In the twenties and the thirties he lived a good deal in Paris. Padraic Colum's *Wild Earth* (poems) was published in 1907. Since then he has continued to write, and today he is producing plays, poems, and articles with extraordinary energy. Arthur Griffith it was he claims who introduced him to literature and he has written a fine life of Griffith published in 1959. He is the last of the writers of the Irish Literary Renaissance. Today he lives in Dublin for part of the year, and the rest of the time in New York. Pádraic Colum is the co-author with his wife of *We knew James Joyce* from which portions of the material used here are taken.

Arthur Power: Is pleasantly indefinite about date of birth; but old enough to have savoured the atmosphere of Edwardian Dublin and to have been a

Eugene Sheehy: B. 1883. Ed. Belvedere. Called to Bar 1910. Volunteered European War, served Royal Dublin Fusiliers and Heavy Artillery. Legal Officer, Free State Army 1922–1923. Chief Commissioner Dail Eireann Courts 1923–1924. Judge-Advocate-General 1927–1928. Circuit Court Judge 1928–1954. Chairman Board of Assessors, Military Pensions, since 1954. Publications: *May It Please the Court* (reminiscences), from which portions of the material included here are taken.

William G. Fallon: b. 1881. Ed. Belvedere. President in 1908 of Young Ireland Branch, Dublin, of United Irish League. Original member of Proportional Representation Society of Ireland, 1910. Assistant Secretary of Parliamentary Party's Press and Public Meetings Agency (London and Britain) 1912–1914. Called to the Bar 1920. President, Belvedere College Union, 1926–1927, of Irish Rugby Football Union 1949–1950. Member of the Adoption Board. Publications, in Catholic Truth Society's Historical Series: *Perpetual Peace: A Catholic Ideal* (1918); *Via Romana* (1933).

Padraic Colum was born on December 8th 1881

serving officer in the 1914/18 War. Of landed gentry stock and educated in England at Public School. Invalided out and went to live in Paris. Became friends with James Joyce and knew Hemingway, Modigliani, Pascin and others. Was art critic for the Paris Edition of the *New York Herald*. In 1930 inherited family estate in Waterford and went to live there and work it. Sold it in 1939 to Land Commission and went to live in Dublin. Published *From the Old Waterford House,* a charming evocation of a vanished era, which went into three editions. Became art critic for *The Irish Times*. Also exhibited paintings *The Living Art,* An Oireactais. At present art critic for *The Irish Tatler and Sketch*. Favourite sports, according to himself, were hunting and sailing; chief amusement, artists; favourite beverage, tea.

First published in the Netherlands
Made and printed in Holland by
N.V. DRUKKERIJ BOSCH, Utrecht